The Book of
Fallacies

The Book of
Fallacies

*A Little Primer of
New Thought*

Lynda Dahl
and Cathleen Kaelyn

Moment Point Press
Portsmouth, New Hampshire

Moment Point Press, Inc.
P.O. Box 4549
Portsmouth, NH 03802-4549
www.momentpoint.com

Cover design by Metaglyph
Typeset in Roman
MG

Library of Congress Cataloging-in-Publication Data

Dahl, Lynda Madden, 1943–
    The book of fallacies : a little primer of new thought /
Lynda Dahl, with Cathleen Kaelyn.
        p. cm.
        ISBN 0-9661327-9-3 (alk. paper)
        1. New Thought.   2. Kaelyn, Cathleen.   I. Title.

    BF639.D13   2001
    299.93—dc21   00-052690

Printed in the United States of America on acid-free paper

10 9 8 7 6 5 4 3 2 1

To Stan, Scott, Matt, Marianna, Courtney, Hero,
Rob, and the Committee II . . . with endless love

L.D.   C.K.

✧ CONTENTS ✧

INTRODUCTION

I'm old enough to have witnessed the deaths of several dear friends, family members, and acquaintances. Good people all, with very diverse characteristics. Yet, years ago I was struck by what I recognized as a similar thread woven through many of their psyches, a thread I hadn't noticed previously because I took it for granted as a condition of life. The thread reflected an underlying sadness that life hadn't worked out the way they'd hoped, that there was so much they had to offer that never found the right time or circumstances, that life wore them down more than boosted them up. Then I noticed that that thread, in various colors and weights, wove its way through many of my very-much-alive family and friends—and through me, as well.

I didn't notice any of this until I read a book called *Seth Speaks* by Jane Roberts. The ideas in this book so challenged my beliefs about life and reality that I felt compelled to read more, think more, learn more. So I went on to read dozens of books by Seth and by other authors. And the overriding reason I hung in there, with tenacity, in the face of what seemed to be preposterous ideas, was because most of these books contained one main theme: We create our reality through our thoughts, emotions, and beliefs. In other words, what seems to happen *to* us is caused *by* us—if we change what we think and feel, we can change our life. I eventually came to realize that life isn't meant to be constantly challenging and heartbreaking, that it can be happy, joyful, even magical, if we but allow it.

My actor daughter Cathleen Kaelyn, my creative and research partner in the development of *Fallacies*, was a teenager when I picked up my first metaphysical book. She and I had always been close, our thinking running parallel much of the time, so it was no surprise when she started reading books similar to those I was exploring. Eventually we began swapping ideas, debating concepts, and looking for practical ways of using the information. And practical applications reveal themselves to Cathleen regularly. In my previous books I talk about how she relied on her understanding of the nature of reality to pull her through some difficult experiences—most notably after she was raped and in the creation of her Screen Actors Guild card.

In my case, there is not one area of my life that has not been significantly changed for the better because of my introduction to metaphysical ideas. Finances, relationships, health, you name it. And because it notes my entry point into metaphysics, I mention in all of my books that I consciously created a million dollars a few years after I started practically applying the information. I also left a long executive career in the computer industry and stepped smack into a life of author, president of a nonprofit organization, co-founder of a publishing company, and eventually, radio host.

Except for the author role, my life was shared by my dearly loved Stan Ulkowski, until March 22, 1999, the day he chose to leave this reality for different venues of expression. His death initiated perhaps the most difficult time of my life, and I can't imagine having faced it without this new knowledge. I came to know firsthand that when the mind's understanding about the nature of reality is truly changed, not only do "good" things happen with more regularity, but when "bad" things occur we're prepared to handle them in ways previously foreign to us. Life becomes less painful, more solid, more centered, its potential more promising, more accessible.

The really big news that emerges from metaphysics is that we all have far greater control over what we experience than we've ever thought possible. In fact, if truth be told and understood, on one level of our psyche we have absolute control over what we experience. Not only do we have the ability to steer our lives along paths of our own choosing, we have the directive to do so.

Quite a jump in thinking from that of the man or woman on the street. But, of course, Cat and I aren't alone in our new views; millions of people across the globe are in the same learning mode. And it all points to something of import taking place in this time and space—the development of a new worldview heralded by a major shift in thinking. When such a shift begins to occur in a civilization, the status quo falls under scrutiny. As the shift broadens, the scrutiny becomes intensified, eventually knocking the status quo off its complacent backside into the roiling waters of hard questions and new insights. Over time a new status quo emerges, accepted as fact by a large slice of the world's populace—and civilization never looks back.

.   .   .

If you've picked up this book, perhaps you're no stranger to metaphysical ideas. Like Cat and me, you may have quested to find new answers. And you probably already know that creating the razzle-dazzle, one-time event isn't what it's all about, although that can clearly happen. What we're all really looking for is a day-to-day flow of life that suits our own characteristics and personalities as a whole, is supportive in all ways, and provides an ongoing, ever-unfolding sense of fulfillment. No small accomplishment, to be sure, but one made possible by new knowledge—and application of that knowledge.

In *The Book of Fallacies*, Cat and I hold up to the light many of the accepted, conventional concepts—*fallacies*—and offer in their place significant emerging ideas—*new thought*. We've chosen the ideas that, through their uniqueness and scope, point the way to changes so profound that each of us can, if desired, learn to develop our lives along paths of conscious choice instead of unconscious happenstance. It is our hope that for some of our readers, *Fallacies* will act as a path from the old to the new, the past to the future, the nonmagical to the magical.

God knows the journey is worth it.

1
PANNING
FOR MAGIC

Worldviews don't turn on a dime. They don't turn at all unless contrary ideas bloom in the current garden of thought. And, boy, if there's one thing most of us dislike it's contrarians, whether in the form of people or ideas. Contrarians say that there are alternative ways of viewing the world—and who needs it? The status quo is just fine, thank you very much.

Or is it? If your personal status quo is one in which you experience a life of toil, broken relationships, constant illnesses, or financial difficulty, and if it brings you a glow of satisfaction, then put this book down and simply enjoy the heck out of your life, because it clearly suits you. But, if you have questions or concerns about the status of your ongoing existence, then it's time to dip into the pot of contrarian ideas and find those that possibly make more sense the more they're contemplated. Not that new ideas should be bought carte blanche, but perhaps they can be explored with less hesitation knowing that the tried and true are there to fall back on if the new becomes too wacky.

Don't forget, we're panning for magic. We're looking for the elusive *something* that makes sense of life, that promises a better way, that by nature leads to a lighter heart, a spring in our step, a smile more often than tears. We're looking for the calm underlying our thoughts, a generous peace of mind, a knowing that all is well, all is manageable, all is meaningful, and all is possible. And, yes, we're looking for material well-being, as well.

We're panning for magic, the kind honed of intelligent ideas and touched with veracity. We're not looking for fluff—sweetness and light won't work for very long. What we seek is sustainable through time, something our children and our children's children can count on to help them create intensely fulfilling lives. We're looking for concrete information that we can work with, that ignites our thoughts and fires our imaginations, and can lead to whatever we desire. So we must pan for magic in some out-of-the-ordinary places. After all, if it were where we've looked before, we would have found it by now.

So, in this book we're going to address certain fallacies—ideas that many of us believe are the facts of our reality. And we're going to counter these fallacies with new thoughts—ideas that must be in place if we're to experience true magic as a normal part of our days. Of course, we can't cover every fallacy or present every new thought that would help lead us to a completely new worldview, not by a long shot. We're simply panning for thoughts that, as the book progresses, will show themselves to have practical application. But rest assured, we *will* build the platform from which, eventually, we'll experience personal magic.

.   .   .

Nothing explains the wonders of the universe better than a story. That's where theory's rubber meets the road. That's where we start to grasp the meaning of the words, "You create your own reality." And that's where the implications behind the words spin our heads with possibilities. So, I'm going to tell you some stories. In each chapter I'll tell two tales straight from my life. The inference in the tales may or may not reflect the batch of fallacies being discussed in that given chapter—perhaps the significance of a story, or its roots in metaphysics, will reveal itself at some other point in the book. But by the end of *Fallacies*, all of the stories will make sense to you, and the nuggets of magic found within each will become apparent.

So, without further ado, on to our first illuminating tale of the universe . . .

Twinkle, Twinkle Shooting Star

On a balmy summer evening Stan was reading in bed, and I wandered out to the deck to enjoy the cool air. The star field blanketed the night sky, capturing my attention. What would happen, I thought, if I tried to consciously create a shooting star? I studied the sky, immersed in the stars and my thoughts. How easy is creation? I wondered. If I ask playfully, yet with intent, for a shooting star, can I work in concert with the universe to manifest my desire? What the heck, I thought, I'll give it a go.

After fifteen minutes or so, visits from perhaps five of our kitties also enjoying the evening, and no wondrous display in the heavens, I decided to call it quits. As I entered the house, I thought, *Okay, universe, last chance for tonight.* I turned around to give a final salute to the star field . . . and a shooting star crossed my line of vision.

A couple of weeks later, I tried it again. And the same thing happened. Stan was driving south to Oregon at the time, so I called him on his cell phone, told him what had occurred, and suggested he give it a try. Twenty minutes later, he called back—he'd created his shooting star, too.

Fallacy 1: God is dead.

EW THOUGHT . . . It's true our world reflects dire circumstances and our private lives can hit more walls than seem fair, but that's not because a source greater than ourselves has opted out. Perhaps the seeming lack of caring by our "creator" can be explained by reassessing the nature of the reality we call home to determine what truly makes it function. So that's what we'll do. But be prepared—along the way we will be forced to redefine our present concept of "God," or the emerging picture won't hold together.

Fallacy 2: Consciousness is a by-product of the brain.

 EW THOUGHT . . . The brain is a by-product of consciousness—and so is everything else. Consciousness is all that is. It is primary. And because it's primary, it's in a unique position: Nothing happens outside of it. From it springs all secondary constructions—planets, bodies, events, everything.

So where does consciousness reside? Everywhere. It's primary, how can it not? Everything inside and outside of physical reality must emerge from the stuff of consciousness, yet stay contained within it.

And that, of course, begins our new definition of God.

Fallacy 3: Life discontinues at death.

 EW THOUGHT . . . Consciousness, or "awareized" energy, can't just disappear as though it never existed. It can and does change form, but it can't annihilate itself. And why would it want to? What would be the point?

When the consciousness that encompasses all that is—or, if you prefer, All That Is—created individualized consciousness from itself, each unit of consciousness found itself still held within the whole, still a part of All That Is, but with a curious perception of separation. That perception eventually led the consciousness which became human to define death as "the end of living." But if consciousness is seen as a discrete part of All That Is, the belief that active, vibrant life does not continue after death is illogical. Surely All That Is has a better plan than to consistently and systematically destroy itself!

What All That Is wants more than anything is to *experience*. That's how it expands. So it recycles its multidimensional creations, moving them out of one context and into another. As consciousness which chose, this time around, the physical world in which to develop, we may move on after death into new lives in physicality. Or we could choose to try other venues outside of time and space. But no matter what multidimensional plans are put into action, rest assured there *are* other plans.

Fallacy 4: God answers prayer.

EW THOUGHT . . . To whom are we talking when we pray? To the entity that created and sustains us? If that's the case, then metaphysics suggests we're communicating with our *inner self*—a nonphysical energy gestalt composed of units of consciousness from All That Is. The inner self has a purpose, just as any composite of consciousness units does, and its purpose revolves around us. Indeed, we are extremely important to our inner self. Each of us is an idea construction which has been given physical life by our inner self so that it can expand its own awareness and experience through us. So clearly, then, our inner self has a lot riding on how we interpret and handle physical reality.

When we ask for assistance or call for help, it's our inner self who directly responds. It's our inner self who extends the helping hand, leads us into the "coincidences" that answer our needs, suggests we not give up too soon. Our inner self uses many vehicles for communication, such as dreams, intuition, inspiration, insight, inner voice, and impulses. Without an inner self we could not function in physical reality, since it not only guides us, it keeps us alive by the inflow of its energy. From the balance of body chemistry to the creation of our dreams, all of our bodily and psychic unconscious activity is directed by our inner self. We are a literal part of it, formed in the inner world, yet appearing in the outer world.

That's our inner self, responder to our requests. And how does a request differ from prayer? It's all in the belief system of the person behind the request or prayer.

Fallacy 5: We face the world alone, with only our outer senses to guide us.

 EW THOUGHT . . . Our inner self communicates with us constantly via a set of psychic inner senses. As mentioned above, our inner self has at its disposal any number of ways to get our attention, and does so by utilizing these inner senses. It also uses this set of senses to keep our body functioning, with all of the unconscious activity that that entails, and to create and maintain our reality by the literal translation of energy into matter.

We cannot live in physical reality without an inner self that forms us and replenishes us moment by moment via the inner senses, and then continues communicating with us, through these same senses, to help us over the rough spots of physical reality.

We are never, ever alone. It's an impossibility.

Fallacy 6: Each of us stands separate from all other energy.

EW THOUGHT . . . There is no separation to the energy of All That Is. Period. The boundaries that look and feel like separation are illusory. Each of us is part of the ongoing multidimensional continuum of consciousness. We are All That Is, we are our inner self, we are our physical self. We are the wind, the snow and the rain and the clouds. We are the plants and animals. We are our children and each other. Literally.

Fallacy 7: Fate and luck rule our lives.

EW THOUGHT . . . If we'd like to feel connected to our source, to feel at ease and significant and that our lives are in our own hands, we must understand that when All That Is created physical reality as home station for some of its consciousnesses—namely, you and me—it didn't choose to leave us at the mercy of an uncaring Fate. When we peek around the curtain of creation and view the mechanics behind the manifestation of an event or object, we come to understand just how much influence we really exert on our lives. Indeed, we come to understand the irrelevance of concepts like "fate" and "luck" and realize our own power.

Fallacy 8: *Our world and everything in it is of physical construction.*

NEW THOUGHT . . . Our world and everything in it is of *idea construction*—a pattern or formation of ideas—that is eventually made to look physical. This suggests that physical reality emerges from the world of the psyche and then takes on the appearance of hard elements. It suggests that the world and its objects start life in a mental realm.

What happened is this: All That Is, in its great wisdom, allowed for the creation of infinite *psychological mediums* within itself, mediums that consciousness could then utilize for its own reasons and purposes. These psychological mediums deal only with idea constructions, and from them emerge all realities. So, physical reality starts life as idea construction, and is eventually translated into "hard fact." But so-called hard facts turn out not to be hard after all, for behind the seeming solidity and supposed laws of physical reality are the ideas, or patterns, that give the structure life—and malleability.

Fallacy 9: *Life offers me few real choices.*

NEW THOUGHT . . . We can't be expected to hunker down into a life defined by the times, history, our parents, or anything else, without an escape mechanism available for when we finally decide enough is enough. That escape mechanism is called *probabilities*.

In the nonphysical medium from which our world and our selves spring, there is a storehouse of potential awaiting actualization. Everything that can possibly happen in physical reality resides here in patterns, ready to be filled when beckoned. For instance, at any given moment I might choose to go to the park and strike up a conversation with a stranger. Or I might go to the park and meet a long lost friend, and never start a conversation with the stranger a bench away. I may not go to the park at all that day. I may, or may not, bash into the back end of a Chevrolet on my way to the grocery store, instead. And on a more practical level, I may choose to have money or not, health or not, love or not, et cetera, et cetera, with all gradations in between.

Any of these events constitutes a valid opportunity, or probability, on my part, and can slip into my life with ease. The event I actualize in the framework I call my life will be there because I choose it. The deciding factor as to which event will become my official experience is focus. In other words, because unlimited possibilities surround me at any given time, and because I have free will, I can consciously choose the course of my life by simply changing my focus.

Fallacy 10: There is one world, one reality.

 EW THOUGHT . . . Every probability is destined to fulfill its inherent potential—even those we reject. Indeed, rejected probabilities play themselves out in other realities that run concurrently with those we officially recognize. Remember, what All That Is wants most is to experience, and one way it can gain the greatest experience is to explore all facets of possibility around a given event. Ergo, all choices offered but not officially accepted live on in infinite other realities, infinite other worlds, developing along lines best suited to their potential. This applies to choices surrounding both private and mass events.

So, there are unlimited paths for us to follow and worlds to create. Clearly, then, it would be helpful, individually and as a civilization, to learn to consciously choose our probabilities, rather than accept them by default.

Fallacy 11: There is one world, one reality (revisited).

NEW THOUGHT . . . There is a further twist to the new thought above that explains the way in which we create our individual realities, and how we do it in cooperation with everyone else. And here it is: Each of us exists in our own *space continuum*, created by our inner self outside of time and space, and within it we play out our life.

Remember, the only real existence for any of us—consciousness that we are—is psychological. Sometimes we make an existence look physical, as with the lifetime we're now experiencing, but even then it's actually an ongoing psychological event camouflaged to look physical. A space continuum is where that camouflage is created and viewed. Each of us is assigned our personal space continuum, and in it we create our reality, without interference from any other consciousness. The ultimate in individuality.

But how, then, do we dovetail our space continuum, or reality, with someone else's? Let's say you and I have agreed to experience an ice cream cone together. I create the scene in my space continuum, and you do in yours. Telepathically we agree on the details of the scene: We're outside an ice cream parlor on a warm summer day, sitting on a wooden bench, watching the people stroll by. We agree to the time and date, we agree to see each other in certain clothing, and so on.

During conversation, you call my attention to the color of your ice cream, a soft yellow. But it turns out the yellow you create in your space continuum has more green in it than the color I see. We both agree, however, that the color is still a soft yellow. The reason this slight difference causes neither of us concern is that you'll never see my construction of your ice cream cone, and I'll not see yours, so the discrepancy won't become apparent. Never will I cross over, if you will, into your private continuum, or vice versa.

So, you may choose to see yourself a little fuller around the hips than I see you. I may choose to create a somewhat uneven sidewalk, and yours may look straight-on. Generally, though, the scene will look very similar to both of us. The other people in our pastoral setting will create it in their own space continuums, making minor adjustments as they please.

This, then, is how a civilization is built. A consensus view of world reality is agreed upon outside of time and space, and that worldview is played out in individual space continuums. There is no one "place" that holds the world reality. Indeed, there is no *one* world reality.

Fallacy 12: Our main method of communication is verbal.

 EW THOUGHT . . . Our communication is primarily telepathic. In fact, the space continuum concept depends on it. How else could we all know how to create our scenes so that there's continuity between them? We telepathically agree to set the stage a certain way in our individual space continuums, and then we play out the event, sticking somewhat closely to the accepted design. If any of us chooses to dramatically alter the agreed-upon stage set, we're considered crazy, or delusional, or eccentric, or something that says we're off kilter. And that's why, usually, we don't.

Fallacy 13: Our thoughts are contained within our brains.

 EW THOUGHT . . . Thoughts, once constructed, run wild with purpose in the universe. So what? Who cares? Consciousness does, for starters, because thought activates the creativity of consciousness. What we think, therefore, becomes the building blocks of what we experience.

Here, in essence, is a scaled down version of how creation in physical reality works: We, consciousness that we are, feed our thoughts, attitudes, beliefs, emotions, intent, and focus to a greater aspect of ourself outside of physical reality. That portion of us, our inner self, determines how best to translate what we're thinking into concrete physical events and material objects. It does so by selecting events from a field of probabilities residing outside of time and space that match the focus and intent of our thinking. Through continuous pulsations of energy (i.e., consciousness) into our space continuum from the nonphysical medium, the chosen events enter our physical reality. Whatever objects are contained within these events are then brought into existence.

Fallacy 14: Mind creates matter.

EW THOUGHT . . . Mind does create matter, but not alone. It takes the mind's physical counterpart, the brain, to do the literal translation of incipient idea constructions into matter, and only after the outer senses have perceived the idea constructions. The inner self, via the mind, imprints the brain with an electromagnetic pattern during the infusion of energy into a space continuum, and the brain then gives the pattern, or idea construction, its physical appearance—but not until one of the outer senses has first perceived the pattern. And if it has—Voila! We create a television set. Or a body. Or a tree. Or whatever. So, while the mind holds the idea construction, the idea doesn't get created into an object without the aid of the brain and outer senses.

Fallacy 15: A chair exists as a physical object whether or not it's seen.

EW THOUGHT . . . Perception, the ability to see or sense something, is the spark that ignites a nonphysical pattern into materialization. Therefore, only consciousness with outer senses—which facilitate the ability to perceive—can create its own physical reality. So, for example, as a chair has no outer senses through which to perceive itself or anything else, it can't create its own physical reality.

Which brings up an intriguing point. When we leave the kitchen and no longer see the dishwasher, does it continue to exist? Or when we turn our back on the dishwasher to reach a cupboard, does it continue to exist? In either case, it can't. Its pattern still resides outside of time and space, but the literal object must be seen by us in order to become physical in our private space continuum. Likewise, if we're blind and we touch an object, the part we touch takes shape, but not necessarily the whole object.

And so it goes for the balance of the outer senses: The object we perceive will be created in some fashion, not as a whole object, but as the part that is perceived by the actuating outer sense.

Fallacy 16: Time moves forward, moment by moment.

NEW THOUGHT . . . Linear time is an illusion formed by our brain's neuronal structure, which can only handle one event at a time. All time is simultaneous, but the brain controls and limits our perception and experience of time. Without a brain to insist on the singular and linear placement of events, we'd be surrounded by all possible experiences in the spacious present—and thoroughly confused. So, we set this reality up as a place where consciousness can create experiences, see them played out, view and review their consequences, and make changes accordingly. And the illusion of linear time works beautifully, given these parameters.

But the fact remains that all experiences are flashed out of the nonphysical medium of simultaneous time and flashed into our reality moment by moment, creating the illusion of linear time. There appears to be continuity to our lives, but the reality is there are no successive moments, one following the other. Instead, each moment is inserted, fully formed, into our reality in the blink of an eye—one blink after another after another.

Fallacy 17: *The past, present, and future are clearly delineated.*

EW THOUGHT . . . Simultaneous time suggests that no event exists strictly in the past, present, or future, that all events exist in the spacious present, with only our brains to insist it isn't so. And each event exists alongside any and all other events—and permutations and gradations of those events—that could ever occur in our life.

What, then, determines which of these infinite events will be included in our past? We do, by what we choose to believe. As our beliefs change, so goes our past, because our past is no more concretely formed than is our future: Both are open for new construction. And that new construction can only be based on our thoughts, emotions, and beliefs of the moment—because the present moment is the only time that really exists.

What we choose to hold in our minds now, then, becomes extremely important to both our past and our future.

Fallacy 18: Cause and effect rules.

EW THOUGHT . . . "Cause and effect" doesn't exist as science defines it. And that's because A) time is simultaneous, with no moments following successively one after the other; and B) all probabilities exist in the nonphysical medium, and any one probability can enter our life as an experience, outside of any preordained time line. What has great meaning, though, is where we place our focus in the present moment—that magical moment from which our whole life emerges.

Fallacy 19: Space can be measured as the distance between objects.

EW THOUGHT . . . Space cannot be measured because space doesn't exist. The area devoid of objects, which we erroneously dub "space," is actually a sea of atoms and molecules not yet given form. This sea of atoms and molecules holds the potential to become anything of material construction in the physical realm. So when, say, a dog bounces in our front door, we immediately translate the animal's nonphysical pattern into a physical form (it is, after all, our space continuum and our reality). To do so, we use the always available atoms and molecules. In the same manner, the dog, in its own space continuum, creates us.

Riddle: Does a dog take up space? Answer: No, a dog is a part of space.

Fallacy 20: Physical objects endure through time.

EW THOUGHT . . . Matter is actually consciousness which takes the form of matter as it projects itself into the physical field, filling a predetermined pattern with available atoms and molecules. Matter has no duration. All of our reality is refreshed from its nonphysical origins many times a second, clearly at a rate too fast to be recognized by our body's neuronal structure. The stuff called matter is constantly, spontaneously recreated by a different set of atoms and molecules, and will conform to the pattern requested by consciousness. Because matter is newly created every moment, it doesn't grow and it doesn't age. It only gives the appearance of growth and age, based on what we agree to, and expect to see, in our reality.

Fallacy 21: Walking denotes movement through space.

EW THOUGHT . . . As stated above, matter has no duration. Therefore, a physical body can't walk anywhere, because it has no duration. It's refreshed from nonphysical reality countless times per second, each reappearance being new to the moment, with different atoms and molecules forming the structure. A body can seem to stride forward, but what is actually taking place is more like what happens to the lights on a theater's marquee—they give the illusion of movement. One can walk from New York to Los Angeles and quite literally never go anywhere.

Why is this important? Only because it places under our belts one more concept that tells us how and where real action takes place—in a psychological medium that translates itself into camouflage in the spacious present. And since this is perhaps the most freeing bit of news ever to enter our heads, we'll explore it from many perspectives throughout *Fallacies*.

Blink and Ye Shall Receive

It was a week before Christmas and the house had a festive air. All that was missing was a new chair to fill a certain spot in the recently redecorated living room. I was driving home from a trip north, feeling pressed to the max and wondering just how I was supposed to find time to go furniture hunting before company descended. About twenty miles from home a thought flitted through my very tired mind: Why not swing by the furniture store and give the floor a quick perusal? Oh, sure. I'd arrive there with only about fifteen minutes until closing time, so why bother? After all, the chair I envisioned had to fit some rather stringent criteria, and it was going to take time to find a match. And besides, I was meeting friends for dinner, and needed to hurry home and change clothes. No, I told myself, bad idea.

But the bad idea wouldn't go away. It came back repeatedly, ignoring my thrusts and counter thrusts of objection. As the exit off the freeway to the furniture store loomed, I, for the last time, set the bad idea aside. But instead of continuing on home, in the blink of an eye I changed my mind and pulled the steering wheel to the right, heading through the exit and toward the store.

I entered the store, spotted my chair immediately, bought it, and within ten minutes was headed for the freeway again.

In Summary

All That Is is pure consciousness from which everything else emerges, from realities to spiders. And everything that springs from consciousness stays contained within it; it's impossible for any construct not to be a part of All That Is. It's also impossible for any construct to be annihilated, for the same reason: Everything is a part of All That Is.

All That Is has a strong desire to experience itself in all its forms. Therefore, it creates individual units of consciousness that have the propensity to group together to become gestalts. These consciousness or energy gestalts then form infinite psychological mediums within which various multidimensional realities are created. Physical reality is one of these realities formed within a psychological medium. It takes on the patina of solidity, but is really built of idea constructions refreshed from the psychological medium, or nonphysical reality, moment by moment in the spacious present.

Within nonphysical reality are held all probabilities that have ever, or can ever, occur in physical reality. As they are chosen by earth-tuned consciousness, they become events or material objects within the space/time context. The impetus for their selection is thought. Because all probabilities have the inherent propensity to seek actualization, infinite realities are utilized by consciousness. Therefore, there is not one world—or one body known as a given personality—but an infinite number of them, each with its own set of probabilities.

Each earth-tuned consciousness lives out its life in its individual space continuum, manifesting nonphysical patterns into concrete events and objects via its brain and outer senses. Through telepathy, agreements are made between individuals as to how a given event will look, and then each person constructs their version of the event in the privacy of their space continuum, as they choose to see it. World reality, then, is a consensus reality played out in individual space continuums.

As probabilities are simultaneous, so is all time simultaneous. Past, present, and future events exist as probabilities in the spacious present, and any can be selected at any point in "time." Since probabilities are fluid and time simultaneous, our physical reality is actually fully created anew from nonphysical patterns with each metaphorical blink of an eye. So, nothing in this reality is around long enough to age, because everything is, literally, refreshed countless times per second. What seems to be empty space to our eye is actually a sea of atoms and molecules that is used to form physical objects. As the moments change, the content of a chair, for instance, also changes, being re-created each time with different atoms and molecules from the ever available sea. And based on this constant re-creation and on the fact that each moment is a fresh one, there can be no movement per se. Motion is simply the moments blurred into what seems to be fluidity.

Our collective inner selves are the key players in this saga of continuous creation—they manipulate the energy from the non-physical into physical; they form us and keep us alive through their own unending energy. Without an inner self to care for us, we could not live in physical reality, let alone inhabit a body. And since there is no separation to the self, then we *are* our inner self, just as our inner self *is* All That Is. A multidimensional con-tinuum of consciousness, so grand and alive and purposeful.

Moving On . . .

So that's our first batch of fallacies. We'll refer back to them as the book progresses, fleshing them out more in the context of their implications to creating a fulfilling life. And, the implica-tions are startling. For instance, one thing we'll discover along the way is that life is not just theoretically meant to be reward-ing, but that there is a universal structure in place that assures it.

2
BUOYED
FROM BEYOND

I'll never forget the horrifying death of my best friend from cancer. I was a young woman with no foundation upon which to rest my saddened heart and unrelenting anger. I'd passed through a fundamentalist religious background and into a stage of agnosticism, not yet having recognized metaphysics in any way, shape, or form. Thank God I'll never experience that terrible hopelessness again. Death has taken on new meaning for me now; or perhaps I should say, it has lost its meaning for me now.

Stan's death in 1999 proved that to me. Had I held the belief system of my past, losing the pillar of my life could easily have destroyed me for a time. But I count myself among the lucky now, the ones who know without a doubt that life is a continuum, and that death is but a blip on the lifeline. I know Stan left this reality with other plans in mind, and that I concurred with his decision because I too had other plans to play out. I also know we'll spend time together again, not as the personalities of Stan and Lynda, but as consciousness that shares a deep love and comes together often to explore and express that love.

When we believe life not only continues, but continues with meaning and purpose, we become free to address birth and death, and pre-birth and after-death, in ways seldom contemplated by our culture. Easing of the grief associated with the loss of a loved one is just one example of what results when we free our psyche from old bonds that no longer apply to our new belief system. Our assured safety in the universe is another, as is our faith in our ability to create our life with a pleasant cohesiveness.

But this marvelous new belief system that supports such outrageously exciting ideas can't be implemented without one key idea firmly in place: We are buoyed constantly by the aspect of ourselves that resides outside of time and space. And, we'll never allow ourselves the trust that is necessary to make physical reality consistently work for us unless we A) believe we are part of a greater consciousness that has our best interests at heart—and tries its best to let us know what those interests are; and B) believe that we will return to this greater consciousness after death, to make new choices and set future directions.

So, after our magical story, let's unmask some fallacies that might just prevent us from flying to new heights of trust—trust that ultimately will lead us to the value fulfillment we so strongly seek.

A Christmas Present From Beyond

It was Christmas Eve of 1999, my first Christmas after Stan's March death. Cathleen and I were preparing my home for the guests about to arrive for our traditional holiday party. During our twenty Christmases together, this night held special meaning for Stan and me because it was always celebrated

with family and friends. So, with the festivities un-
derway, he was very much on my mind.

The previous summer I'd sold Stan's red truck,
the one everyone had come to identify with him so
strongly. It was easier for me to get rid of it than to
deal with the deep sadness it engendered those first
few months after he'd left. So now it's Christmas
Eve, and I haven't seen the truck since the day it
was driven away by its new owner. I step out the
front door and kneel down to pet a cat. As I raise my
head, Stan's truck slowly drives by the house. I'm
stunned. My immediate reaction is the same deep
sadness of the summer; my next is one of peace, because I know Stan is with me this Christmas Eve,
after all.

Fallacy 22: *Life is without meaning.*

EW THOUGHT . . The universe is meaningful.
Everything that is contained within the universe is
meaningful. Each creature has its own purpose and
meaning, both as part of the overall universe and on a personal
level—and each creature's personal meaning meshes with the
greatest good of all others.

The universe is intimate and subjective. Everything happens
for a reason, and every action changes the universe. We *are*, in
fact, the universe.

Fallacy 23: Our spirituality stands apart from our human characteristics.

 EW THOUGHT . . . While we are in physical reality there is no division between the mental, physical, and spiritual: They are, literally, one. After all, can the multidimensional self be divided? If we think there is a delineation, then we don't understand spirituality or the nature of reality. This results in our creations being less than fulfilling, and at times downright frightening. For if any of the three—mind, matter, or spirit—are separated, in our mind, from the others, our creations will reflect this separation. Indeed, it's a prevalent condition in today's world—the fallacy of separation, the fear it engenders, and the results of that fear.

Fallacy 24: We must grow into our spirituality.

EW THOUGHT . . . As literal parts of All That Is, we are spiritual, by definition. We are not cut off from God; we have not done, nor can we do, anything to cut ourselves off from our source. Metaphysics suggests a grander design for our existence that has nothing to do with traditional ideas of spirituality.

In a nutshell, All That Is, in its intense desire to experience itself, creates units of consciousness from itself that are imbued with characteristics similar to its own. One is a great desire to fulfill itself through creativity; another is free will.

Together, these two characteristics give each consciousness unit the ability to organize, expand, and develop along any lines it chooses. Most development takes place once a multi-dimensional consciousness gestalt is formed, which is a merging of infinite individual units that hold the same underlying purpose. In the case of humans, each of us is a multidimensional consciousness gestalt with a purpose—a purpose that cannot help but emerge from the basic spirituality of All That Is.

Fallacy 25: My existence has no direction.

EW THOUGHT . . . Please reread the last sentence of the previous new thought before proceeding.

Okay, so here we are—a multidimensional consciousness gestalt with a purpose. But what purpose? In general terms, it's threefold:

> To reach toward *value fulfillment*
> To learn to *manipulate energy*
> To work on *personal issues*

Value Fulfillment: Every unit of consciousness created by All That Is is imbued with a psychological and physical propensity, called value fulfillment, that propels it forward, in search of fulfillment, by way of individual as well as group development. The act of constantly striving toward fulfillment, then, is a characteristic and purpose of all consciousness. And that, of course, includes each of us.

Manipulation of Energy: Our thoughts, attitudes, beliefs, focus, and intent, translated into energy, create our reality. Physical existence is in place for consciousness which wishes to explore the manipulation of energy through the manipulation of thought and feeling. Each of us chose this medium in order to learn the intricacies of energy movement, and the ramifications of such movement, by seeing our creations laid out in what seems to be a time line based on cause and effect.

Personal Issues: Each of us is eternal consciousness which constantly seeks new venues for growth. We like to specialize on our direction, focusing on certain aspects of personality or character that we feel bring us the most fulfillment. Therefore, we select some of our private or personal issues before birth with the clear desire to work them out to our satisfaction.

Surely that's enough direction for any lifetime.

Fallacy 26: *God will direct my path.*

 EW THOUGHT . . . Over the millennia, humanity, in general, didn't know who was creating what, and in its ignorance assigned the role of power to its god of the day. Metaphysics, on the other hand, puts the ball clearly in the individual's court. It says that each human being's job is to monitor outside reality, make decisions and choices based on what it sees, create and experience the results of those decisions, and change what doesn't work. This being so, let's substitute "inner self" for "God," and see where it takes us.

As discussed in chapter 1, our inner self is the multidimensional consciousness gestalt which formed us and keeps us alive in physical reality. While the inner self doesn't call all the shots in our individual realities, it does hold the pattern or blueprint for what we hope to accomplish in this lifetime. Difficulties arise when our outer self sets goals significantly divergent from its inner purpose. When this occurs, there is virtually no way the outer personality can gain any kind of true fulfillment from living.

However, when our inner self and outer self are in concurrence as to our purpose this time around, a balance occurs. The necessary enlightenments are made known to our outer self, and as we act on them and experience their results, a more solid relationship grows between the inner and outer portions of our personality. Advantageous circumstances open, and we are more able to clearly ascertain the truth of what we're experiencing, instead of simply accepting the camouflage covering the exterior. As a result, we tend to transmit undistorted data back to our inner self for processing, and this data may become part of the pattern of an upcoming event in our life. What will the event look like? Who knows? But one thing is for sure, it will reflect the balance and trust experienced between all portions of our self.

So who directs the path? Call it a joint venture of heroic proportions.

Fallacy 27: *To reach my inner self I must meditate and practice spirituality.*

NEW THOUGHT . . . The belief that our inner self is something apart from us that must be wooed through our good intent is just another holdover from old religious ties. The truth is our inner self is an active, interested participant in our life every moment of our day. It monitors our thoughts constantly, and furnishes us with insights galore. All we have to do to develop a conscious awareness of, and interaction with, our inner self is listen to our thoughts, determine which thoughts have come from our inner self as impulses, intuitions, or insights, and then use our thoughts to talk to our inner self. It's true, meditation or a light altered state of consciousness does help quiet the mind and calm the outer self, which helps considerably when first attempting to hear our inner self, and later when we may want to explore broader psychic realms. But is it necessary? In a word, no.

That said, however, it can, indeed, be very enriching to reach our inner self on far deeper psychic levels by using an altered state. Remember, we are multidimensional beings, not simply physical beings. Most of our self is outside of time and space, and a lot of action takes place there that can only be tapped when we bypass the conscious mind completely. So, it's not that the deeper psychic state doesn't have great value; it's that a life of fulfillment, one where the outer self and inner self are in harmony, can be led by simple awareness of the inner self and a desire to communicate with it naturally and normally throughout our days.

Fallacy 28: *I am insignificant in the scheme of things.*

EW THOUGHT . . . Our inner self needs our outer self as much as the other way around—and this point cannot be overstated. Without our exterior self's outer senses in place to translate energy patterns from our inner self into physical events and objects, the inner self could not participate in physical reality. And since part of its value fulfillment (i.e., growth) comes from just such participation, we do our inner self a favor by being born into earth life and working hand-in-hand with it to create the next scene and the next. We are, therefore, extremely significant in the scheme of things.

Fallacy 29: *Coincidences are the exception, rather than the rule.*

EW THOUGHT . . . Our days are loaded with magical moments orchestrated by our inner self. We only notice a few of these gems and then, usually, toss them off as "only coincidence," ignoring their inherent magic and the help they're sending us.

In fact, the universe runs on so-called coincidences. Coincidences hint at an underlying organization to events that, if revealed, would boggle the conscious mind. This organization is intimately and personally tuned to our needs and desires, and suggests a most precise focus in our direction by the universe. The universe recognizes us through the building of our life via coincidences. We are important to the universe, or it wouldn't turn in our direction.

Fallacy 30: Logic is all I can trust.

EW THOUGHT . . . If we assume that the intellect is the only source of decision-making information available to us, we experience a life that presses and stresses us far more than is comfortable. By not trusting our inner self, and the help it offers us, we can send our stress-to-success ratio off the charts. Sure, we may reach our goals, but if we believe we're alone, that we have to figure out and control every tiny detail of gaining and then maintaining our goals, we'll pay a very high price, indeed, for that success.

We simply don't know all that our inner self knows about the situation at hand—it set it up, for goodness sake! While we see a moment point in time, our inner self sees all probabilities surrounding that moment point, and all of their repercussions. So, what may seem like an illogical impulse to us—such as the sense to go left when we think right is where it's at—can make the difference between reaching our goal with ease, reaching our goal with stress, or not reaching our goal at all.

In fact, the type of information we need to magically maneuver in physical reality comes in many guises. Perhaps we experience it as a direct knowing, or as an intuitive opening, or as a phrase that plays over and over in our mind. Maybe we resonate with a slogan on a billboard. But come the information will, singularly or in groups of insights and impulses over time, because it's the job of our inner self to give us all the help we

need to make a go of this lifetime. And it's our job to
the information when it arrives.

It wouldn't hurt to ask for it once in a while, too.

Fallacy 31: Faith is nothing more than a strong belief in something.

EW THOUGHT . . . Faith is the glue that holds
everything together. It permeates the universe.
We should applaud All That Is for filling the universe with the substance of faith, because without it, our
universe couldn't function for even one second. Faith is an
active ingredient that magnifies those desires that are in
alignment with our greater good and individual fulfillment.
It removes impediments from our path, and promotes the
best life possible for each of us. And further good news is
that when we exhibit just a little faith (the size of a mustard
seed, perhaps?), the universe takes over and adds to it
mightily, helping us along as a matter of course.

The catch is, we have to have faith in order to experience its
bounty. So our watchword for this lifetime: Keep the faith.

Fallacy 32: My thoughts are private, unless I choose to make them known.

EW THOUGHT . . . No Privacy Act in the world
will keep our inner self from knowing each and
every thought and feeling we generate. That's its
job—to know exactly and precisely what we think and how we

feel. It needs to see the trends in our thinking, it needs to know when we instantly change our mind about a situation, or how far we are into the process of altering a belief. It needs to know what makes us happy, and what we expect from, say, the upcoming board meeting we're worried about. From our thoughts and feelings it will assess our reality, see if the physical picture matches our thinking, and, if required, alter the exterior to meet the interior.

And when we talk about whether or not thoughts are private, let's not overlook communication with our very physical friends and family. Remember we're basically nonphysical energy gestalts existing in a psychological medium that looks like hard fact. Our method of communication occurs far more through telepathy than we've ever realized. So, outside of time and space our thoughts are heard loud and clear, but by the time they're received in physical reality by all concerned, they've become more a sense of our intent than individual thoughts. In other words, our intent, which manifests first in our thoughts, is what people consistently pick up on, if not on our direct thoughts—although clearly that can happen, too.

Fallacy 33: Problems and challenges reflect a soul not fully developed.

 EW THOUGHT . . . A lack of challenges leads to a lack of growth. This holds true for any realm in which we find ourselves. Growth—or value fulfillment, as it's more accurately called—comes from expanding our understanding, and challenges help perpetuate new understanding. Thankfully, there are no fluffy white clouds upon which to place our backsides and opt out of experiences. That's not to say our problems have to break our metaphorical backs with their weight and force, or that we need to be bombarded with them continually. Rather, we're supposed to be learning how to handle problems with ease and assurance, and create problems less haphazardly. Regardless of knowledge, no life is without its challenges.

Fallacy 34: *Striving for perfection is what it's all about.*

 EW THOUGHT . . . Perfection suggests definite endings. Consciousness suggests continual beginnings.

Fallacy 35: *Dreaming is an offshoot function of the brain.*

 EW THOUGHT . . . Dreaming is a primary function of consciousness. The dream state is the flip side of waking reality, just as real and just as necessary to maintaining physical reality. In the most protected area of sleep, deeper than the dream state and not traceable through brain patterns, we participate in two separate activities. The first is a passive state in which we're given information to absorb and concepts to study. It's here that, for our consideration, our inner self gives us alternatives to those beliefs that are undermining our ability to create a fulfilling life.

The second activity in which we participate in this protected area of the dream state is an active one. Here's where we take what we've learned in the passive state and play it out through participation and examples. In conjunction with all other earth-tuned consciousness, including the animals, we try on probabilities for size and fit, and then select some of the ones that will enter physical life as private and mass events. This state is also used to rejuvenate the body.

As we return to a less "distant" state of consciousness, we enter the normal dream state. Often the symbols created here are representative of the information we've absorbed earlier in the deeper dream state.

Fallacy 36: After death I lose my identity to the greater part of me.

EW THOUGHT . . . While we certainly become aware of our stature within our inner self when we leave physical reality, and expand our knowledge and awareness because of it, our personality is not homogenized into the whole, erasing the lines between it and our inner psyche. We formed our unique characteristics on our own, sometimes through hard work, and we deserve to keep them intact. And so we do—unless, that is, we decide to develop them further after death, in nonphysical reality, which is an option open to us.

So, while we probably won't focus on this lifetime's personality after death, nuzzling it instead into a cozy corner of our psyche along with the other earth-tuned personalities we've created and experienced over "time," it will always be there for our remembrance, exploration, and further development.

Fallacy 37: I get to relax after death.

NEW THOUGHT . . . After death, we might relax for a while, but then it's back to stretching toward value fulfillment. We might choose to return to physical reality with a different body and personality, even a different sex, but with some of our "old" characteristics generally in place. Then our purpose would be to develop and strengthen those characteristics and add new ones that enhance the whole. And, as always, our primary purpose would be to deal with problems of manipulation and physical construction of energy.

If we've worn out our desire to continue in physicality and our inner comprehension has reached an exceptional level, we might choose to become an inner self. That means it's time to grow our capacities beyond what we feel we can do as an earth-tuned personality, by creating other earth-tuned selves that then develop their own desires and capabilities. They, then, will feed their experiences back to us for contemplation and learning—just as we do today, for our inner self. Multidimensional learning for multidimensional consciousness.

Fallacy 38: *Evil exists.*

 EW THOUGHT . . . Evil is a concept. Like any concept, such as goodness, evil will take its manifested place in physical reality if called upon by the thoughts of earth-tuned personalities. Given the nature of All That Is, evil is not and cannot be a separate force.

Fallacy 39: *"White light" protects my house.*

 EW THOUGHT . . . The only protection needed from anything is complete faith and trust in a safe universe and a supportive inner self. The use of white light or any other property or ritual to secure a physical structure is, then, redundant. (It's also indicative of a belief in an unsafe universe.)

Dreaming a Message

About two weeks after Stan died I had a dream. Cathleen and I were in an upscale department store searching for a gift for Stan for the approaching new millennium. The store was about to close, and I was feeling more and more anxious because no gift had presented itself to my awareness. The dream started fading and the transition to the awake state began.

Then I heard the clear, strong words: "Your gift to Stan is your love and your happiness." Certainly, he has my love, and always will; I decided in that moment to do everything I could to rebuild my life to a point where I could offer him my happiness, as well.

Thanks to my inner self, and its message to me in that time of dire need, I was able to focus my mind and emotions on something concrete, something life affirming, and get on with getting on.

In Summary

There is no objective, impersonal universe. Everything that happens in physical reality or anywhere else is laced with purpose and meaning, and is experienced by the whole. Every action changes the universe, because every action is contained within All That Is—and All That Is *is* the universe. Consciousness is a multidimensional continuum of All That Is, indivisible. Therefore, we are mental, physical, and spiritual creatures of consciousness, created by our inner self and contained within All That Is.

As a literal part of All That Is, our existence obviously has significance. We are each a consciousness gestalt with a purpose. Generally, that purpose is threefold: to reach toward value fulfillment, to learn to manipulate energy, and to work on personal issues. To help us develop that combined purpose is the job of our inner self. It holds the blueprint for what we wish to accomplish in this lifetime, and constantly sends us reminders as to what that might be—and how to get back on track, if needed.

Since we are an extension of our inner self, then staying in touch with it is easy. It's as close as our thoughts, because it uses our mind and inner senses to send us the information and assistance we need to make a go of physical reality. While there is no need to be in an altered state of consciousness in order to communicate with our inner self, sometimes it's helpful. But if we wish to tap into the deeper realms of our multidimensionality, then an altered state becomes necessary.

Because our inner self sees all probabilities surrounding our moment point, it's advisable to develop a conscious awareness of the information that comes from it to us via our inner senses. We can't possibly know the implications inherent in a situation as well as our inner self does, and by listening, sensing, and watching the coincidences at play in our life, we'll discern directions and possibilities perhaps completely overlooked otherwise.

Even with this superb assistance, though, we still will meet problems and challenges. Growth is the name of this game, and there is no growth without the solving of problems. The value of a close conscious interaction with our inner self is that it can help us make the challenges less far-reaching, and more easily solved.

And don't forget who chooses the challenges: We each do, partially during the deepest part of the dream state, in a protected area not traceable through brain patterns. It's here we try on probabilities for size, and then make the selection as to which ones we'll meet in physical reality as events. We don't do this selection alone, however. Not only is our inner self the one who sets the stage for this deep dream-state work, but the inner selves of all other consciousnesses, including the animals, join in in some form to select probabilities that will be played out on a global, mass-event level.

It would be a shame, at death, to erase all this learning in which we participate while alive. So we don't. While we certainly become aware of our containment within our inner self, and go on to other types of experiences, we are not forced to obliterate the boundaries that delineate our past personality. The characteristics of that lifetime stay intact, as they do from all lifetimes, and can actually be developed further after death, if and when we choose.

And, we have other options of growth open to us after death, as well. For instance, we can be born into another lifetime with a different personality and possibly a different sex, but still with some of our "old" traits at play. And, if our inner comprehension is considered exceptional, we can even choose to become an inner self, tackling our growth, or value fulfillment, from a whole new perspective.

So the beat goes on . . . from one venue of expression to another, a multidimensional continuum of consciousness contained within a safe universe where evil is simply a concept and faith a literal reality.

Moving On . . .

In the first two chapters we've explored general fallacies about the nature of reality, and some new thoughts about who we are, from whence we came, and why. Hopefully a picture is developing that suggests a far more meaningful existence than most of us have been taught. But there are many pieces of the pie still to be discussed, so let's move on to the wonders of the mind and its enormous participation in the creation of our individual realities.

3
THE GOLD
CALLED MIND

When I started studying metaphysics, perhaps the biggest surprise to me was the concept of the mind's incredible role in the universal scheme of things. Sure, I'd read the requisite books about the power of the mind, with their suggestions on how to use it to become successful, prosperous, and so on. I'd listened to motivational speakers extol its virtues by means of inspirational stories, and audiotapes on the subject filled my nightstand. But until I got into metaphysics deeply, I didn't know half the story.

I simply didn't realize that the power of the mind stems from its basis outside of physical reality, that without it being anchored safely in the nonphysical, no physical reality could exist. The power of the mind is literally infinite, because it springs from consciousness that is literally infinite. And because of its infinite power of creation, we're able to experience the fruits of physical reality—the ripe as well as the spoiled fruits *we create*.

All of the magic of life starts with the mind, and ends with the mind. Everything delivered to our doorstep is there because of our mind. So, if we're looking for golden opportunities that will help us lead exceedingly fulfilling lives, we have no further to look than our own mind.

The Morning After

My partners in a new company were at my home one evening during its pre-launch formative days, hashing out both intricate details and broader ideas. One major issue struck discord within me, and caused such a heated discussion amongst us that I silently wondered if perhaps I should back out of the partnership. Later I lay in bed reviewing the evening. I finally asked my inner self for guidance and fell asleep.

The next morning I chose from my closet an indoor jacket I'd not worn for well over a year. I put it on and stuck my hand deep into one of the pockets. My fingers touched an unknown object. It was a stick-on label with the name of one of my partners embossed on it. I didn't recall having seen the label before. I studied it, thinking about the request I had made to my inner self for guidance, and decided not to voice any concerns about the direction of the company until I saw how that day's continuing meeting would play out. I also wondered if my named partner wasn't somehow the key to a resolution.

A couple of hours into the session, this partner broached a new subject with such creativity that I thought perhaps that was the input that I had sought. But, while this new subject did play a part, she didn't bring the big news to the table until mid-afternoon. What she suggested then made it all click, and I knew immediately where we were headed and why.

Interestingly enough, the new information had nothing whatsoever to do with our discussion of the previous night.

Fallacy 40: *Mind is a function of the brain.*

 EW THOUGHT . . . The mind supersedes the brain, coming before it and after it. In fact, the mind, which is multidimensional, creates the brain as the vehicle through which to function once it enters physical reality.

Remember our discussion in chapter 1 about the inner self, and how each of us is an idea construction projected by our inner self into physical reality? Well, our inner self doesn't cut the lifeline between it and us at birth. It actually extends itself into physical reality *through and as our conscious mind*, using the conscious mind as the receiving station for the data it wishes to bring to our attention. And that's why, as discussed previously, our inner self is as close as our thoughts, at times planting ideas in our heads, and at other times listening to what we think. A shared mind, a shared reality.

With this close association comes abilities we're only beginning to tap into and understand, because it turns out that we have powers of creation similar to those of our inner self. And the shared mind is what gives us access to those powers.

Fallacy 41: *Consciousness is a function of the mind.*

 EW THOUGHT . . . Consciousness is not something we possess; consciousness is something we are. Therefore, consciousness is not a function of the mind. The mind, actually, is a function of consciousness.

Fallacy 42: Life's events are happenstance.

EW THOUGHT . . . The beauty of physical reality is that it's ours to do with as we please. As consciousness, we're here to learn to manipulate energy. We do it by selecting the probability we wish to experience, turning the probability into idea constructions, and then manifesting those idea constructions into physical reality by manipulating nonphysical energy. Our multidimensional mind plays a significant role in this very non-happenstance process.

First, the outer portion of the mind assesses external reality and draws conclusions from what it sees. These conclusions, or perceptions, take the form of thoughts, attitudes, beliefs, and emotions. Some of these perceptions are accepted as fact by the outer self. When that happens, the conscious mind steps in and takes these "facts," or beliefs, and sends them to the inner self. The inner self's job, then, is to select probabilities that best suit what the outer self believes, and mold them into idea constructions. These idea constructions enter physical reality as patterns imbedded in the energy pulsed into physical reality moment by moment by our inner self. The outer senses and the brain then perceive the idea constructions in the physical world.

To reiterate, a continuous loop is in effect: outer self perceives outside world; outer self forwards its perceptions to conscious mind; conscious mind forwards outer self's perceptions to inner self; inner self sends same perceptions back to physical reality as idea constructions imbedded in energy; the brain, via the outer senses, translates idea constructions into events and objects in the outside world.

No happenstance, simply universal logic.

Fallacy 43: The ego is Peck's bad boy.

EW THOUGHT . . . If any part of the human personality has taken a bum rap, it's the outer self—also known as the ego. At times it's seen as the overbearing part of us, the out-of-control portion of the personality, the part that's necessary to tame and subjugate if we're to become spiritual or whole. It's the part that supposedly leads us astray and causes more trouble than it's worth. But the ego has been misunderstood. The ego's *reaction* to its beliefs has become its *definition*.

Sitting on top of the conscious mind, if you will, is the ego. While the job of the conscious mind is to direct daily activity and make decisions, the ego's job is to feed the conscious mind perceptions about the outside world so it can make those decisions. The ego is firmly focused outward, assessing the "truth" of the events of its life and then reflecting on its truths, or beliefs, with enough strength that the conscious mind is forced to deal with them. The conscious mind, in turn, deals with the ego's input by feeding it to the inner self without sprucing it up. The inner self then creates the reality that the ego expects to see—and its truth is made manifest, like it or not.

Fallacy 44: The ego has a destructive bent.

EW THOUGHT . . . The ego has come to believe that it stands alone in life, with no direct, daily ties to anything beyond it. Even if it believes in some concept of a god, usually that concept comes replete with suggestions of immense separation between the lowly human full of failings and the spiritual being full of light. So, the ego starts thinking it's the end all, the place where the buck stops, the singular bearer of all of life's burdens, and sometimes the cause of them, too. It starts seeing itself as an insignificant, detached island in the sea of humanity, with no deeper purpose or meaning than to survive, no matter what it takes, until the point of death—and, depending on its philosophical beliefs, possible annihilation.

This scenario becomes the working model for many of the egos of earth-tuned consciousnesses, this fear-based mindset that can eventually lead to a very destructive bent. In the last new thought, we said, "The inner self then creates the reality the ego expects to see—and its truth is made manifest." It's not so difficult, then, to understand the state of today's world, is it?

Fallacy 45: The subconscious rules.

EW THOUGHT . . . Psychoanalysis has made quite a place for itself based on the idea that the subconscious is a hidden lair of hampering impulses and deep, dark secrets normally blocked from the conscious mind. The information stored there supposedly holds answers as to why our life is in a shambles, so we seek professional help—lots and lots of professional help, if we can afford it.

The multidimensional mind, as we said, is an extension of our inner self into this reality. Our inner self holds all the information we'll ever need to participate in physical life: personal material, such as memories, family information, et cetera; racial and species history; and all information pertaining to the universe as a whole, and physical reality in particular—such as how realities are created and the camouflage and mechanics used, how planes of existence come into being, how energy is transformed, and so on.

This massive amount of information is not, however, assigned to the conscious mind. Much of it is stored in the unconscious mind, the storage area set up by our inner self for data not needed on a daily basis. But, this information is fully accessible by the conscious mind when asked for or needed. The problem is, we must believe it's available, or it becomes invisible to our conscious nature.

So, our unconscious mind is unconscious only to the extent that we don't ask it to, and then believe that it will, share its wealth with us. Once we ask, the unconscious information we request becomes conscious, and very nonmysterious and nonthreatening. Indeed, we find it to be most useful.

Fallacy 46: Mind is a clean slate at birth.

 EW THOUGHT . . . The mind is well stocked with thoughts, attitudes, and beliefs before it integrates with the physical brain. It holds desires and intents and objectives given it by the inner self as a framework for the life it will come into. This sets the stage for challenges and opportunities ahead. And why the prebirth mind-stocking? Because one purpose of our being in this reality is to learn energy manipulation and physical construction translated into life experiences, and our inner self wishes to point us in a certain direction out the chute, so to speak, which could help fulfill our intricate individual purposes.

Fallacy 47: I am what I am.

EW THOUGHT . . . We are what we think we are. We're not that way "just because." We're the way we are—a reflecition of illness, health, bliss, or despair—because we believe something about the condition we experience. Looking outward, we perceive the inward, because the creation in exterior reality can only mimic the creation in internal reality.

Fallacy 48: I am incapable of changing my life.

EW THOUGHT . . . Let's define beliefs as *strongly held thoughts*. Further, we'll say they are seldom questioned, so sure are we that they are fact. And then we'll add that they create our reality, because our inner self listens to what we think of ourselves, our world, our outlook on life, and everything else we hold beliefs about, and then runs with our assessment. That means it will choose probabilities to match our beliefs, and in will come a life event that mirrors those strongly held thoughts.

You are very capable of changing your life. We all are. It simply means changing our mind about some of the beliefs we hold near and dear to our hearts.

Fallacy 49: Facts and beliefs are not the same.

 EW THOUGHT . . . Facts and beliefs are absolutely one and the same in this reality we call home. Don't forget, physical reality is cast in a psychological medium. Even the supposed laws of physical life, such as gravity, are simply beliefs all earth-tuned consciousness has agreed to agree to—ergo, they become the framework for our reality, but they are nothing more than accepted beliefs made to look physical.

Fallacy 50: Some beliefs cannot be changed.

 EW THOUGHT . . . If the whole of our civilization decided to suspend the law of gravity, gravity would be no more. However, you can see how improbable that idea is—not because it's beyond the possibility of happening, but because few of us in physical reality could buy into the belief long enough for it to take hold, so strong is our acceptance of gravity as a law outside of ourselves. Ah, but when we change a personal belief about our inability to make money, or be healthy, or be happy, then there is nothing to stop us from making it come true.

Fallacy 51: Our emotions are contained within our minds and bodies.

NEW THOUGHT . . . Emotions cannot be contained within any structure, any more than thoughts can. Once generated, emotions come alive with purpose. They produce symbols in different stages of our awareness, from the physical to the soul level, at times becoming concrete material items, at other times becoming psychological realities.

Take our physical world—a living room, for instance. Depending on how we're feeling, the facade of that room will alter. If we're depressed, the walls may actually come closer together, restraining us as our depression restrains us. The lights may dim, the colors darken. If we feel great happiness, we tend to create our objects with firmer lines and more vivid images. Either way, our feelings are accurately translated into the symbols of our physical reality.

And at the soul level, they're translated into psychic realities that are then explored for meaning and expression by our inner self. They become highly charged psychic structures representing inner realizations that have not been captured through direct comprehension. At times these emotional structures become symbols we utilize in our dreams, with the hope of bringing unconscious comprehensions to the conscious mind, so we can deal with what's behind them.

It's very important that we understand the nature behind emotions, because when we allow ourselves the knowledge of their impact, we can more easily decipher the psychological meaning behind our manifested idea constructions and dream symbols. If we never give our emotions and feelings the benefit of being deeper and more meaningful than the surface suggests, we've cut off one more avenue to understanding how we literally created a past event, or how to consciously create a future one.

Fallacy 52: Emotions just happen, with little inducement from me.

EW THOUGHT . . . Emotions don't happen in a vacuum; they are generated by our beliefs. They are always a result of what we think. We may not see the connection at the moment of emotional impact, but with a little sleuthing the cause of our emotions will become apparent.

Fallacy 53: I seldom can control my emotions.

EW THOUGHT . . . Emotions can and should be consciously managed. They hold tremendous power, because they start the build up of creative energy that will eventually translate itself into an upcoming event in our life. Beneath almost everything we encounter in physical reality lies emotion, emotion generated by us and tied to beliefs we hold. Since our beliefs create our reality, when we learn to control our emotions—that is, manage them by transforming them into different emotions—then different beliefs will come to the forefront. And that's what we're after—the ability to select the beliefs we wish to experience, and then bring them to fruition through our managed emotions.

Fallacy 54: Our expectations in life are formed by our experiences.

NEW THOUGHT . . . From our thoughts, we choose our beliefs. From our beliefs we generate emotions. From our emotions we generate expectations. And from our expectations—which are strongly held beliefs about outcomes not yet made physical—we create our life. Expectations are the end product in the creative chain. Because the result we desire is so assured in our mind, an expectation has enough energy behind it to spark events into existence.

Meanwhile, the ego analyzes its life experiences with little understanding, if any, as to how they were actually created. So, the ego naturally comes to the conclusion that experiences happen, expectations arise out of the experiences, and a belief system is formed from those experiences. Totally skewed from the reality of the matter, though, and quite unproductive thinking when we wish to consciously take control of our life.

Fallacy 55: Desire should be sublimated.

NEW THOUGHT . . . Desire is the prelude to expectation, and since expectation is the fuel that propels our goals into physical reality, we should cultivate desire consciously. It's a wondrous tool at our disposal. But be aware, if desire does not reach the level of expectation, then it's for naught. Desire alone won't actualize an event or physical object. Nothing short of expectation, or assumption, will work such wonders.

Jamming On . . .

Thanksgiving eve, and I'm stuck in an Interstate 5 traffic jam two hours from home. My car has moved perhaps two miles in forty minutes. I'm angry and frustrated, feeling trapped. Actually, I'm wallowing in the feelings. No surprise the traffic doesn't move.

Okay, girl, you know the drill. Change your emotions, change your reality.

Oh, shut up and leave me alone. I'm tired and all I want to do is get home. I'm not in the mood for metaphysical mumbo jumbo.

Up to you.

Okay, okay! (Geez, isn't anything ever easy in this reality?)

So, I start working with my emotions. Calming them down, setting them aside. Then I start visualizing the traffic breaking free, my car picking up speed, feelings of relief and perkiness kicking in. Shortly thereafter the car inches forward enough for me to spot the next exit, which I know has a restroom nearby. Slowly, very slowly, I reach the turn off, take care of business, and call Stan from a pay phone to apprise him of the situation. He says, wait a minute, it just so happens I drove the back roads of that area not long ago, and I think there's a bypass you can take. He checks the Oregon map, tells me what to do, and I'm on my way.

The side trip added about fifteen minutes to my normal drive time, but that day, according to the newspapers, it saved at least an hour, perhaps two. Seems there was a major accident about ten miles north of my restroom exit, and traffic didn't move for a long, long time. So while I didn't break free by staying on Interstate 5, as I'd visualized, another probability opened up that still allowed me to meet my goal—which was to get the heck home at a reasonable hour.

In Summary

Our multidimensional conscious mind is an extension of our inner self into physical reality. Since it is an actual part of that consciousness which forms us, it clearly supersedes the brain, coming before it and after it. Information flows two ways within the mind: from the inner world of our inner self to the outside world; and from the outer world of our ego back to our inner self. Although the mind is not actually divisible into parts, for discussion's sake it can be imagined as three-pronged: the unconscious (or subconscious) mind, the conscious mind, and the ego.

The unconscious portion of the mind plays the role of warehouse, tucking away all information we may ever need in order to be sustained in physical reality. Little of it is sent to the conscious mind at one time, because the conscious mind only needs, and can only handle, the data it is manipulating at the moment. As the conscious mind needs more information—or specifically asks for it—the unconscious mind reacts and sends it posthaste. The key to living a rewarding life is found in knowing that material can be accessed and utilized that heretofore was believed to be off limits to the ego.

The ego sits atop the conscious mind, and is a conglomeration of beliefs and perceptions. Through these filters it determines its stance in life, and feeds its reflections back to the conscious mind and on to the inner self. The inner self takes the ego's perceptions and translates them into the personality's physical life. What the ego sees, the ego gets. That the ego created the exterior world in the first place is usually lost on it. A cycle then exists that must be broken if the personality wishes to change its life. The ego must start to think differently, and view the world differently, in spite of what it sees. Eventually, then, its exterior world will reflect its new beliefs and attitudes.

The physical world is made up of materialized beliefs. Some of them, like gravity, are accepted as mass beliefs and reflected as "laws" in earth life. Others are personal, such as the belief in victimization. But no matter the belief, they are all legitimized in the psychological medium we call physical reality. They show themselves as events, objects, and bodily conditions. Seen as facts, they are simply beliefs.

Emotions have the same power as thoughts: They are imbued with the ability to create. They become symbols for us, both materially and psychically. They enter our reality as broken objects and events, or stimulating objects and events, depending on which emotions are in action. And at the soul level, they are translated into psychic structures that the inner self then deciphers for comprehensions far beyond ours.

From our emotions, which emerge from our beliefs, we generate expectations. Expectations are the final thrust that brings an event or object into our reality. Without expectation of some sort backing it, the probability we desire is closed to us. To get what we want out of life takes an expectancy, a trust, if you will, that we can move forward in our chosen direction. Of course, we move forward due to our expectations, anyway; but it would be nice to do it with finesse and conscious choice for a change.

So, from the ego to the conscious mind to the unconscious mind to the inner self and back again—a flow of multidimensional consciousness without division, only made to look partitioned by our inability to grasp the totality. A flow of multidimensional consciousness that literally creates our reality. The ultimate magic.

Moving On . . .

So far, we've only touched briefly on the mind, but we'll pan for more of its gold before we end *Fallacies*. For now, let's remember that everything that occurs in this reality is due to something we think. So, creating a life of comfort and pleasure comes down to how we manage our mind. Even our bodies are not immune from our thoughts—but that's part of the story found in the next chapter. See you there.

4
The Body Unimpeded

In *Oversoul Seven and the Museum of Time*, author Jane Roberts states that "miracles are nature unimpeded." So is good health, I believe. Maybe miracles and good health—and all things that flow effortlessly into our lives—are simply nature unimpeded. If we look at nature through a broad lens, one that contains our bodies, our world, our reality, and the reality outside of time and space—indeed, all of All That Is—then how could anything be outside of nature? And since All That Is doesn't impede itself, it can be assumed that if an impediment occurs, the culprit looks back at us from our mirror.

But we also have to assume that even a stumbling block that we identify as our own is part of nature. It's not a failing, or a lack of (fill in the blank). It's simply a lack of clarity in our belief system. Illness, disease, accidents, pain are all natural expressions of our inner framework—and sometimes just the thing needed to bounce our minds and spirits into new, refreshing territory. A magical jump-start, if you will.

However, pain is pain, and not too many of us consciously seek it out for the pleasure it brings. What we do consciously seek is a way out of it, or perhaps a way never to get into it at all. If you're in the last category, then clasp the hand of metaphysics, because there is no other philosophical or psychological system in the world that explains the nonphysical genesis of pain and offers options to creating it in the first place.

The wondrous news in metaphysics is that we create our own reality. God bless All That Is for allowing such creativity, because it's open-ended: What we create, we can alter. The catch is, we must believe it. We must believe in the magic of our body, our mind, our inner self. We must believe that the nature of personal reality encompasses the framework through which we not only can, but do, control our lives.

So, after our magical story, let's see if, with the next batch of fallacies, we can strengthen that belief in our awesome creativity.

Believing Is Seeing

Before going into meditation early one morning, I decided my underlying purpose would be to feel myself become one with the universe. So, after a few minutes of settling in, I saw myself drop the camouflage pattern of my body and become a field of energy that merged with the energy of the universe. Later, when I was "reassembling" myself into body form before I ended my meditation, an unusual thing happened. Some of the energy coming back into my camouflage pattern headed specifically for my right eye and highlighted it for a moment. I was startled, since I hadn't consciously directed it there.

I've worn glasses or contact lenses for over forty-seven years. The previous week I'd had an eye exam and the doctor had upgraded my prescription. The morning of my meditation I had inserted a fresh pair of weekly disposable contacts, and as I came out of my altered state of consciousness, I wondered about the darn things. Oddly, everything in mid-range was a little blurry, although my vision had been clear as a bell since I'd left the doctor's office days before. Was there a defect in this newly inserted pair of contacts?

For a week I fought the out-of-focus lenses, wondering if my eyesight would return to normal once I disposed of the current pair of contacts in favor of fresh ones. But at the same time, I wondered what, if anything, had happened during that meditation. I have a strong belief in assistance from my inner self, and I knew I'd lately broadened my outlook on life. Was this change reflected in my vision? Seeing more clearly, perhaps?

After I replaced the old set with a new one, and my eyesight didn't improve, I'd had it. I visited the doctor that day. He ran his checks and told me he was altering my prescription. He said he felt a muscle in my eye must have relaxed and caused a change in vision. "Which eye, doctor?" I asked. "And is its sight better or worse than on my previous visit?" Sure enough, it was my right eye, and the vision had improved.

Fallacy 56: There is a mind, body, spirit connection.

NEW THOUGHT . . . There is far more than a mere connection between mind, body, and spirit: They cannot be separated. They are an integral package, the spirit and mind made manifest in the physical body. To delineate them muddles the picture, distorting yet again the nature of consciousness. True, it's sometimes necessary to discuss them individually, for clarity's sake, but once the discussion is closed, the parts should be, in our mind's eye, integrated back into the whole. They must be, if we are to absorb the intricacies of the multidimensional soul.

Fallacy 57: The body is a stand-alone molecular structure.

NEW THOUGHT . . . Our body is not simply a system of mechanics and chemistry. It's a living energy gestalt formed and maintained by our inner self and inhabited by our personal consciousness—which is part of our inner self. Our inner self fills in the body's nonphysical pattern moment by moment with its energy translated into flesh and blood, and then controls its automatic responses, such as breathing and heart beat, and the balancing of its chemistry.

So, the body cannot stand alone, in the truest, most literal sense of the words. It can't do anything, in fact, without our inner self's constant support.

Fallacy 58: *The body is composed of flesh and bone.*

 EW THOUGHT . . . On the outer level, the body is composed of flesh and bone. On the inner level, the body is made of sound, invisible light, and electromagnetic properties which form a nonphysical pattern around which flesh and bone coalesce. This nonphysical pattern is highly susceptible to our thoughts and emotions. Always before the body responds to stimuli, the inner pattern has already reacted, and actually initiates the later physical reaction. In other words, by the time we experience motion, activity, illness, or any other kind of phenomenon, the show is virtually over.

Fallacy 59: *Identity is dependent on the body.*

 EW THOUGHT . . . Just as with any physical object, the pattern for our body is constantly refreshed from the nonphysical medium by our inner self. The atoms and molecules that make up our body this instant are not the ones that will form it in the next. Yet our identity doesn't change moment by moment. That's because our identity is a psychic organization that actually resides outside of time and space and goes on ad infinitum, with or without a body to anchor it. So, no, identity is not dependent upon the body.

In fact, if you've ever had an out-of-body experience where you consciously left your body behind while exploring your bedroom or neighborhood, the question of identity depending on your body probably became moot.

Fallacy 60: *My thoughts have little influence on my body.*

EW THOUGHT . . . Each thought we think produces an inner sound that has a significant effect on our body. And the sound affects not only our body's atoms and molecules, but the organs composed of the atoms and molecules, as well. In essence, we speak to our body with the sound of our intent. If the sounds we produce are discordant, the results to our body are discordant. That's why a repetitive negative suggestion can be so injurious to our health and well-being.

Fallacy 61: *The body is vulnerable to outside influences.*

EW THOUGHT . . . Our body is vulnerable to our beliefs. Through our beliefs we may choose to impact our body by using an outside influence. In catching a cold, for instance, we allow the outside conditions access to our body. That's the only way detrimental conditions can enter our life. We create our own reality, including the condition of our body, based on our thoughts, attitudes, and beliefs.

Our inner self always strives to maintain our body's health and equilibrium. When blocked from its task by our thoughts and beliefs, it's forced to supply what we demand, which could translate into a world of hurt. "Protecting" our body, therefore, means changing our beliefs about its vulnerability.

Fallacy 62: *Viruses attack randomly.*

 EW THOUGHT . . . Viruses must be invited to attack; they can't make the choice on their own. In fact, so-called harmful viruses are always present in the body. They remain benign unless triggered into action by our beliefs or emotions.

Fallacy 63: *My present disease can be traced from my past.*

 EW THOUGHT . . . Time is simultaneous: The point of creation is the present moment. From this moment the past is structured. The events of the past are chosen from the probabilities in effect now, and they're selected based on our beliefs. Thus, a sudden belief in illness will insert into the "past" experience of the cells the biological cause of today's disease . . . and we can prove it was there all along because the doctor discovered it in 1975, remember?

The cells of our body take their cue from our thoughts, and alter their existence accordingly. Therefore it is far more accurate to say that cells react to what we expect to experience in the future, rather than what we did experience in the past. So you just might say that cells precognate, forming their past and setting their future in this very moment.

Fallacy 64: Heredity starts the process.

NEW THOUGHT . . . Consciousness creates form; form does not create itself. The data found in the genes and chromosomes are impressed on them from within, prior to birth, by the consciousness about to become physical. It chooses the kind of body it wants to inhabit, and designs its cellular structure accordingly. Heredity doesn't start the process; the process is started when our consciousness decides on a generalized line of experiences it wishes to explore and puts some of the pieces in place before birth.

Fallacy 65: Heredity rules.

NEW THOUGHT . . . Like everything else in physical reality, hereditary leanings, once defined by our inner self, are not necessarily sacrosanct. Take supposed hereditary heart problems, cancers, and other physical ailments that are not birth defects but ghost images of possible future creations. Until they are spurred into action by our thoughts, attitudes, and beliefs—most likely by our expectation and acceptance of the so-called hereditary path—they remain probabilities, nothing more. Some so-called hereditary traits may never change, because we chose them for a purpose—which is not to say purposes can't be reconsidered during a lifetime.

Fallacy 66: *The blood of my parents runs in my veins.*

NEW THOUGHT . . . If the body is made anew moment by moment from outside of physical reality, and if atoms and molecules different from the ones used in the last iteration compose this moment's body, the notion that we carry the same blood as our parents and other relatives is a fairy tale. Once the egg and sperm come together to become the vehicle for consciousness wishing an earthly experience, no other physical structures related to our parents are ever within us. True, we may carry some of our parents' bodily characteristics, such as their blood type, but the actual blood has no association with the past. There is no past blood—or past anything.

Fallacy 67: *Man evolved from apes.*

NEW THOUGHT . . . The concept of evolution says there is a progression of physical development and change over a given time line, moving the species from the past into the future. However, in a framework where time is simultaneous and events are selected moment by moment from probabilities in the nonphysical, there can be no evolution, as we've come to know it. What happens is that a species is precognitively aware of changes it wants to make, and so alters the present state of the chromosomes and genes to match what it wishes to experience, preparing itself for its next developmental step. In essence, cellular comprehension straddles time.

As always in this reality, there is never a predetermined future based on a given past.

Fallacy 68: *Once an illness starts, it must run its course.*

 EW THOUGHT . . . There is no "course" for an illness; it will stop when we're ready to end it. How could it not? Even if it appears that a past illness ran a certain course, the course was still of our choosing and of our approval, right up to the point of elimination.

Interestingly, we often halt an illness before it even becomes apparent to us. The cause of the budding illness is brought to our conscious or unconscious attention by our inner self, and by changing certain conditions in our life, with or without knowing why but in response to the input from our inner self, the budding illness is remedied.

Fallacy 69: *Certain diseases can be eradicated.*

EW THOUGHT . . . As a mass consciousness, we put diseases into play that reflect what we feel, anticipate, believe, and fear. And diseases are idea constructions. Once an idea construction has been thought into existence, it cannot be removed from potentiality. It can lose its significance to mass consciousness, and therefore its focus and strength, but it still exists and can return any time we choose to bring it back into our current reality. So, if the disease happens to be polio, for instance, eradicated or not, it can return again and again.

Fallacy 70: Spiritual or faith healing is miraculous.

EW THOUGHT . . . All healing is miraculous, in that a reversal of a condition or illness is the result once the desire of the person involved reaches a certain pitch and their expectation takes an upswing. In essence, the personality decides it's had enough, and so creates the tools it will accept as healing agents. Whether those agents be priests, medications, sulfur water, witch doctors, or the personality's own visualizations doesn't matter: The ill person will have created the scenario which allows healing to occur—some scenarios are just more dramatic than others. But healing is never brought about by an outside source. Symptoms can be cured for a given illness by drugs and so on, but if the beliefs that caused the illness aren't dealt with, either the same symptoms will return or another illness will develop.

Fallacy 71: Illness can cause death.

EW THOUGHT . . . Illness may be the technical cause of a death, but it is never the perpetrator of it. Death is always our prerogative, and the choice of how to die is up to us. So, of course, is the timing.

Fallacy 72: Death, by nature, suggests a massive assault to the body.

EW THOUGHT . . . Leaving this reality doesn't have to be traumatic. In fact, it can be as simple as a slowing of the body's processes and a gradual disentanglement of mind from flesh; or, if we choose, a sudden but natural stopping of the body's processes. If death weren't so frightening and mysterious, our race would automatically follow these and other options open to it at the time called death. But since our experiences follow our beliefs, most of us find ourselves in troubled straits, indeed, at this crucial time of transition.

Fallacy 73: Body energy is limited.

EW THOUGHT . . . We need to replenish our physical energy daily through nutrition and rest, but energy never runs out. That's one of the many things our inner self does for us—supplies us with unlimited energy every moment of our life. That we don't take conscious advantage of such an amazing fact is usually based on our lack of knowledge that it's even possible.

Fallacy 74: The body is a lower vibration than the spirit.

EW THOUGHT . . . It's true that the body and inner self's energy have a different rate of frequency, but different doesn't mean less than. A throwback to old religious beliefs, the body is seen as somehow degraded, a thing we should aspire to shed. In fact, many of us still believe we must deny the flesh in order to progress spiritually.

But, the body is an extension of our inner self into physical reality. It's an idea construction designed and developed by that loving consciousness, not only so the ensuing personality can enjoy physical life, but so our inner self can, as well, through its very intimate creation. So, to say the body is less than the inner self is a complete misunderstanding of the nature of consciousness.

Fallacy 75: If we're spiritually evolved enough, we can live in this reality without a body.

EW THOUGHT . . . A consciousness without a body can visit here, but it can't stay for long. This reality is meant to support consciousness within a given physical framework, and that necessitates the use of the outer senses to create an individual's perception of reality—and, in turn, having outer senses necessitates a body. Nonphysical consciousness doesn't have the tools of creation needed to survive in physical reality, so it can only make a quick appearance, and then only if invited. Like an event or object, non-earth-tuned consciousness can't just show up in our private space continuum without our conscious or unconscious permission.

Tooling Care Free
Through Life

A funny thing happened on my way through my fifties. I awoke one morning to the realization I'd passed through menopause without even knowing it. I'm not talking about symptoms coming to an end and it finally dawning on me. I'm talking about no symptoms at all, except the end of my menstrual cycle.

While I've never had any serious illnesses, I've had my share of colds, flu, menstrual cramps, headaches, back problems, and the like over the years. But by the late eighties even these had dribbled to inconsequential. By 1990 I'd not been to a doctor for almost five years (and haven't since), so I dropped my health insurance. I've taken no over-the-counter drugs except cold tablets since the late eighties, and basically keep only Tylenol, first aid cream, and Band-Aids in the house. At the point of writing this, I've not been ill for easily three years, and this time frame includes the sudden death of my beloved Stan—a time in which illness might be expected.

I have unfailing belief that my body knows exactly what it's doing in regard to keeping me healthy. I have unfailing belief that there is no disease or illness that can touch me, unless I request it. I have unfailing belief that there is not a reason on God's green earth I must suffer pain. And, most importantly, I have unfailing belief in myself and my ability to monitor my thoughts and emotions and place them in a context that keeps my mind and body relatively peaceful—not always in top form, perhaps, but able to rebound quickly.

And I thank metaphysics, from the bottom of my heart, for showing me an alternative structure of reality that suggests a freedom I never previously dreamed possible.

In Summary

Our inner self extends itself into flesh to create and experience the richness of physicality, its color and sensations and essence. It does this by creating a personality, and then selecting bodily characteristics for that personality through which to focus on certain kinds of experience. From the moment of psychic conception until after the point of death, our inner self never leaves our side. How can it? It's a literal part of us. It keeps our body alive by controlling its unconscious processes, and constantly feeds us all the energy we need, not merely to sustain life, but to enjoy it to its fullest.

While the body is composed of flesh and bone on the physical level, it has an inner pattern that supersedes the flesh and bone, and around which the physical properties are constantly, moment by moment, formed. This pattern is composed of invisible light, sound, and electromagnetic properties, and is highly influenced by our thoughts. Before the body shows an alteration of any sort, from losing weight to healing a fracture, the inner pattern has already reacted—otherwise the change could not occur.

Our identity is not dependent on a body. First, the body is not one continuous object. It is refreshed from nonphysical reality more times than we can count per second, and with each renewal different atoms and molecules become part of the structure. And, second, we started life as a multidimensional gestalt of consciousness long before our body was formed, and that is what we will always remain. The body does us the very much appreciated honor of being our vehicle through which we can experience this particular life in a physical environment. In fact, we can't reside in this reality without a body, because we need its outer senses to translate idea constructions into material objects.

The condition of our body is a reflection of our thoughts, attitudes, beliefs, focus, and intent. While our inner self strives to maintain our body's health, it still has to deal with our beliefs. And by the nature of this reality, come what may, our inner self has to impose the results of those beliefs on our body. So, an illness has no preset course to run. It will simply come to a natural conclusion once we've determined we're through with it.

Since there is no past or future per se, our cells form their condition in the now. Actually, our cells react to our beliefs about the future (even the future of the next ten minutes), and insert into the past conditions that make the present and the future look like the *effect* of the past. And this applies to evolution as well as inconsequential illnesses: The cells precognate the future, and prepare themselves to meet that future.

While heredity does play a part in our makeup, it doesn't have the influence we often assume. In fact, it's *assumption* that brings about certain "hereditary" conditions, not necessarily the propensity toward the condition itself. After all, it's belief, emotion, and thought that manage the state of the body—far, far more than has ever been credited. And that includes when and if we allow healing to occur. What we believe about ourselves, our predicament, our god, our goodness (or lack thereof), and so on, will determine which healing agent we will select to work for us.

Illness doesn't cause us to die; we cause ourselves to die, at times by choosing a certain illness. If we better understood the nature of this reality, choices other than traumatic modes of dying would become obvious to us. For instance, we could gradually disentangle from the body; or we could stop the body's processes immediately, naturally, painlessly.

The bottom line: How we view the world and our participation in it, and the beliefs we hold that back those views, will in large measure determine the health or illness of our body. Altering a bodily condition requires a mental change. That change will be followed by its physical reflection. No exception.

Moving On . . .

Mind, body, and spirit—at this point, we've covered them all. Hopefully you don't see them as separate, but as a psychic composite of consciousness formed from the inside out. The miraculous nature of physical reality supports and encourages such composites; indeed, it is set up specifically to welcome them. And when they arrive, in the form of you and me, the consciousness behind physical reality is ready to help us design the most interesting, compelling lives we can handle.

And that's just what our next chapter is about.

5
BRINGING IT
HOME

I can't tell you how excited I was, how my mind swelled with possibilities, when I first encountered the same ideas you've just read in the first four chapters. I could barely sleep through the nights, and I waited impatiently for the moments when I could return to my book bag during my normally busy days. I was a manager with Apple Computer at the time, with over fifteen years in the computer industry. The only other time I can remember experiencing such flat-out excitement at learning new ideas was when I took my first computer programming class in the late sixties. I embraced the logic of flowcharting with an intensity of focus and thrill that rocked, and eventually radically changed, my world.

Logic has been a key word with me since those days long gone. I loved the sense of clarity that settled on my mind when I thought a situation through logically. And now, having become intimately familiar with my inner self and its gentle guidance, I love and appreciate even more the free-flowing mixture of intuition and logic that has replaced the more linear approach I embraced as a young woman. Far fewer brick walls and much more happiness, I'm here to tell you.

But this new mixture wasn't easy for me to achieve. While the metaphysical ideas I was reading touched a deep intuitive chord, I was left with little to hang my logic hat on. And that made me uneasy. The solution, my mind said, was to use the information to consciously create a goal, something I desired, something I could point to and say, see, I created that because of my new knowledge of the nature of reality. And I did accomplish my goal in that, as I mentioned previously, I created a million dollars several years after choosing it as my first serious attempt at conscious creation.

So, while theory is stimulating and mind expanding, unless its practical ramifications can be seen and applied, we may as well read an encyclopedia. In this final chapter, therefore, we'll take some of the ideas covered previously and view them through different lenses. This time, we'll discuss some of the practical implications, and throw in a few how-tos for good measure. While there is no certainty of what you, our readers, will do with what you learn, or re-learn, in *Fallacies*, we'll at least highlight some of its implications before we turn you loose to experiment for yourselves.

The Bagel Bag Caper

A year prior to Stan's death, he and I started planning a large conference in New York. When he died, the conference was three months away. But, as it was important to many people, I decided to go ahead with the event.

The third night of the conference was a special dinner and entertainment of sorts, and I was to be on stage through much of it. I packed a long silk dress

---

of soft gray, white, and muted rose for that evening, one I'd worn six weeks before to my son's wedding. Along with the dress, I included a jewelry case that held a Tahitian pearl necklace and earrings that Stan had given me on my birthday the month before he died. I didn't bother to check the case for the earrings when I packed; I assumed all was well, as I'd not had occasion to open it since the wedding.

But before the dinner, I opened the jewelry case and discovered one earring missing. I felt sick at heart. This can't be, I thought. I can't allow this probability to be the final one. So standing there, I did a hurried visualization, put on another pair of earrings, and joined the crowd in the ballroom. Later that night, I returned to my room and prepared for bed. While reaching to turn off a lamp across the dresser from my jewelry case, something caught my eye. There, lying on a half-empty bagel bag, was my "lost" earring.

Fallacy 76: The cards are always stacked against me.

 EW THOUGHT . . . The universe leans in our direction. We must set aside all the trials and tribulations we've experienced in life, all the horror stories told to us by others, all the heartache and pain we've seen on TV and in the papers. We're not denying the validity of such experiences, but we're going to finally get a grip on the fact that *none of those experiences were caused by an outside agency*—not by God, fate, luck, or another person. They all came from within the active participants in the events, and mostly from simple ignorance about the nature of reality. The universe does not—repeat, does not—stack the deck against any of us. Ever. We do it to ourselves.

This point cannot be downplayed. To do so leaves us wavering between faith in the workings of the universe and doubt about the veracity of it all. Without faith, we see a dark side, an insecurity to life, instead of a beautiful opportunity to hone our existence along paths of conscious choice—all the while receiving incredible universal support. The safe haven and peace of mind are found within faith; doubt creates the brick wall. After all, we get what we believe, remember?

So, how do we start to build awesome faith in the universe and in our ability to interact with it on a minute-by-minute basis? The answer to that question isn't simple, because it's so individualistic. In my early days of metaphysics I took on the concept of conscious manifestation in hopes of proving to myself the truth of what I was reading. I intently focused on consciously creating certain events and objects. As I describe in my previous books, I started by trying to create simple things that I didn't have great stake in achieving, but that might happen often enough to beat the so-called odds. My greatest early successes were with parking places, and eventually, with a high "hit" ratio behind me, my mind was primed enough to cautiously step into other realms of conscious interaction.

One such interaction I enjoyed developing was asking the small voice in the back of my mind for yes/no answers to all kinds of questions, and then teaching myself how to clear my mind and emotions so the answers wouldn't be distorted. Eventually I built up to hearing one or two words, and now I can hold a short back-and-forth dialogue with my inner self. If I'm emotionally strung out or have too much riding on the answer, then I sometimes color the information, if it comes through at all. But without a budding faith in the nature of this reality, I couldn't have opened that doorway to my inner self—distorted though the information may be at times—because the possibility would never have entered my mind.

Some of my friends choose to work more internally, if you will, in their quest for faith. Several have developed the ability to become lucid at will in the dream state. Others have taken lucid dreaming to the max by learning how to do conscious out-of-body projections. Still others have tried channeling, or have become very comfortable with automatic writing or the Tarot. And one of my friends has become an expert at spotting the underlying significances that dot his day in the form of serendipity and coincidences.

But the bottom line is that once you start stretching toward your inner self with an open mind, no matter your vehicle or technique, your inner self will respond—and your trust will increase. As the days go on, opportunities will present themselves that will lead you to trust in the universe more and more. And, if you allow it, that trust will magically spill over into other events and areas of your life, until finally you'll feel safe, assured, and peaceful in your version of physical reality.

No bogeyman, no fear. Free at last. One step at a time, my friends, one step at a time.

Fallacy 77: The laws of nature are unbreakable.

NEW THOUGHT . . . If any supposed law of nature is broken by anyone, does the law exist—or is it simply a cherished mass belief that we momentarily allow to be suspended? The fact that this reality is created by our combined inner selves in individual psychological mediums made to look physical suggests that all "laws" are psychological constructs. And being psychological constructs, or idea constructions, means they are always malleable.

Take the weather, for example, a force supposedly outside of ourselves. Can it be impacted by thought? Ask the hundred-plus people who attended a conference in Seaside, Oregon, in April, 1994. It had been raining for four days, but they were determined not to cancel their marshmallow roast. So, they consciously created a cloudless circle over their hotel and adjoining beach and enjoyed their bonfire—rain free. Later, within ninety seconds of ending their fun for the night, the rains came again.

This type of interaction with nature is possible because nature is not outside of us. Mass thoughts, therefore, have great impact on local and global weather patterns. The patterns respond to the thoughts, emotions, and expectations of the populace. But individuals can impact the weather in their personal reality, too. Try it some time. Wish for the sun to peek out from behind the clouds, hold your focus of thought, put some energy behind it, and imagine it happening. I'm quite good at materializing rainbows, when I put my mind to it. Play with your own creativity and see what power you hold.

Remember, our reality is literally constructed anew with each moment that passes. That gives us the opportunity to play with supposedly immutable laws and alter their effects. My

pearl earring on the bagel bag was the last in a string of supposedly lost jewelry that returned to my reality, and objects
other than jewelry have at times followed the same pattern. And
I'm nowhere near alone in this type of experience. It's almost a
yawn nowadays to hear stories of returned items, because it's
happened to so many people I know.

Yes, natural laws can be broken, because they aren't really
laws.

Fallacy 78: Time marches forward.

EW THOUGHT . . . Time marches forward and
backward. And sideways. And inside out. Which is a
whimsical way of saying that time is far more malleable than we've come to believe. Remember, it's the brain's re-
sponsibility to organize events that reside in the spacious present
into what seems to be a from-birth-to-death line of experience.
Once we understand that, we can play with time, move things
around, and our brain will acquiesce to the new time line.

For instance, we can pull an event from our so-called past,
reshape it through our thoughts, and insert this newly structured
event into our memory flow—literally altering our official past
by adding to it. It's not that we've eliminated the original past
event, we've mitigated its impact by diluting its strength (or
adding to it, in the case of a pleasant past event). I've done it, as
I relate in *Ten Thousand Whispers*, and many of my friends
have, also. While each of us experiences a different strength of
impact in the present from such an alteration, we do experience
an alteration.

And while you're playing around in the spacious present, why not choose to meet a probable future self? Determine in advance what you want out of life, from where you wish to live to what your home will look like. Then, in an altered state, ask your inner self to start a movie running of what that life will be like. Let your inner self fill in the details. And if you like the future life you're seeing, bring it alive by consciously applying thought, intent, and focus to it in your day-to-day life.

Another fun thing to try with the spacious present is to sense the probabilities around a choice you must soon make. For instance, if you're debating between two job offers, go into an altered state and ask your inner self to help you recognize the probabilities inherent in each choice. Then listen for input, and try spontaneously writing down your thoughts. Also watch your waking reality for signs and clues that fill you in on the probability streams connected to the two jobs. Be sure to listen for answers and direction from your intuitions, impulses, and dreams, too.

Don't forget, the events in the spacious present aren't restricted to ones affecting this lifetime. Past lives, and future ones, reside there, too. Try going into an altered state and asking to be made aware of a past life (future lives are more difficult to access for most people, because their inner self may deem it inappropriate for them to know too much about the subject). You'll probably get snippets of scenes, or flashes of the costume of the day, or maybe an emotional response to something that occurred in that life.

Simultaneous time and probabilities. Combined, they are one of the most freeing concepts we'll ever discover.

Fallacy 79: Life is a patternless flow of events.

EW THOUGHT . . . Life is an intricacy of significances, laced together as beautifully and quietly as a spider's web. We translate into physicality from the vast field of possibilities that which is significant to us. Patterns for anything and everything exist, and all it takes to bring a given pattern into our life is turning our focus toward it. That tells the universe that now our intent has moved from experience or object A to experience or object B.

For instance, when our car mirror is broken, we may turn our thoughts toward replacing it, and then take action that will be in alignment with the result we wish to experience. Our inner self hears that we want to manifest an auto glass shop in our reality, and that we've located an address we wish to visit. It then sets the wheels in motion, so that when we leave our neighborhood and enter High Street, there's the auto glass shop just where it should be. Of course, there was High Street just when we expected to turn on to it, too, and there was our neighborhood when we walked out the door, and there was the phone book when we opened the drawer, and . . . Although the auto glass shop, the street, our neighborhood, and the phone book existed as patterns in the nonphysical, they didn't exist for us until we turned our psychic attention to them, and trusted they would be there. We choose, via our thoughts and trust, our next significant moment, and it's pulled from the field of possibilities and made physical.

So, think about it. Do you focus on all the possible pitfalls to every potential action? Are you afraid for your life, or your child's life, every time you turn around? Do you project fear into the future like an unfurled banner, proclaiming your belief in it? And knowing what you know now about the nature of reality, do you think there's a strong probability of meeting that fear, if you keep giving it significance and backward trust?

Remember: Our life's events flow with purpose from what we focus on, what we assume is real, and where we place our trust.

Fallacy 80: *The energy behind both positive and limiting beliefs is neutral.*

NEW THOUGHT . . . Energy is never neutral. It's a positive force, ever inclined toward creativity and fulfillment. Therefore, nonlimiting and limiting beliefs don't carry the same vitality. Those beliefs that lead to a happier life are more in keeping with the natural leanings of the universe, so they grab hold more quickly in the field of probabilities and expand at an accelerated pace. Limiting beliefs meet certain resistance, for they're not in keeping with the overall creative framework. Usually this means they must be held in our thoughts with repetitiveness before we meet their results in life.

Our mental patterns, then, become very important. To make any significant changes in our reality, we have no choice but to see ourselves for who we really are, and that necessitates knowing intimately what we think. So we must learn to watch our thoughts and identify our beliefs. One way to do this is to keep an eye on our emotions, because behind every emotion is a belief. Try following your thoughts outward from your emotions, and see if you can find the end of the trail—the belief or beliefs that are creating the emotion. Start making a list of what you find on these sojourns, and then make up your mind to change what limits you.

Until we know ourselves from the inside out, we'll continue to run on autopilot, letting our beliefs take us where they may, instead of setting our own course.

Fallacy 81: Beliefs are difficult to change.

EW THOUGHT . . . As discussed in chapter 3, a belief such as gravity is difficult to change because of the strong mass belief in its existence— we've agreed to it, en mass, as a "fact" of our physical reality. But the garden variety of beliefs which form the framework of our life, beliefs such as "I am a poor money manager," are not necessarily hard to change. The belief that such statements are true is what may be more difficult to change, because we don't see the statement as a belief, we see it as a fact. But beliefs are nothing more than assumptions held closely to our hearts—we've accepted them so heartily we don't question their veracity. And that's what causes so many of our problems.

Hey, we've lived it, for heaven's sake! Every time we turn around, another situation arises that "proves" the statement is hard reality. Oh, yes, it's definitely a fact of life, not just some silly words that simply bounce around the inside of our mind: Illness cannot be escaped; I'm not worthy of love; It's a big, bad world out there. These are facts, too, not beliefs. Right?

Because of the beliefs we hold, we often block solutions to problems. If we believe, for instance, that we're an ineffective parent, a solution to the latest family teen crisis may not show itself until we set aside the sack cloth and ashes. So, one way to clarify our beliefs is to write down what we see as fact, and then realize that everything, every single item on our list, is simply a belief.

Fallacy 82: It takes time to change a belief.

EW THOUGHT . . . To be accurate, we don't really change beliefs (although we'll continue using the term); we select new beliefs that we'd prefer to hold and withdraw our attention from those that are limiting us.

As far as the time it takes to change a belief, remember we reside in a psychological medium made to look physical. And also remember, all action happens in the non-time-limited, nonphysical reality before entering physicality as an event or material object. In actuality, then, since we're only working with a concept in the mind, we can change a belief instantly. In practicality, however, it may take a while. When we believe we're accident prone, we've probably proven it to ourselves many times over, and the idea that we can easily change the situation seems contrary to the facts of our life. But, with some knowledge and practice, changing beliefs becomes easier—and faster.

That said, examples of instant belief changes abound in our lives, and we can identify them if we just think about it a little. Something brought us to a point of saying, "No more. I'll not accept this. It is no longer an option." And we simply closed it down and went about our business, free from its effects. I've done it with illnesses before, and I'll bet you have, too.

Fallacy 83: Beliefs are held in our mind as thoughts.

EW THOUGHT . . . We not only hold beliefs in our mind as thoughts, we also hold them as visual images. In other words, some of our beliefs are attached to mental pictures we've assigned to them. And one image may stand for one belief, or several. So, when working with beliefs, watch for a picture to flash in your mind, and try to tie it to a given belief. Then use imagination to consciously change the mental picture, thereby releasing the belief from your field of significance.

Fallacy 84: Visualization works.

EW THOUGHT . . . Visualization is an incredibly powerful tool, because it sets an image in our mind, and holds it there. By the nature of this reality, that's pretty potent stuff. But no matter how many visualizations we do toward a selected goal, if we hold conflicting beliefs around that same goal, and we're unwilling to address them, we may as well pack it in. The good news is that visualization by itself can at times alter our beliefs with no conscious effort from us, simply because the visualized goal is eventually taken for granted—then, expectation has entered our picture, and we're in a new ball game.

But let's assume our beliefs are in alignment with our goal. Why then, technically, might visualization work for us? Because there is a definite connection between images and materialization. Mental images are extremely powerful because, by nature, they seek definition in the physical world. When we create an image in our mind, it's composed of invisible light, sound, and electromagnetic properties, just as is the pattern for a physical object. That means the mental image is indeed incipient matter, and so will attempt to reproduce itself in physical reality. Our imagination pushes us into untried territory, imbuing that territory with potential life. The combination of imagination and expectation can bring about almost any reality within the range of probabilities.

So, how does one go about consciously changing the weather, materializing lost jewelry, ending an illness, or creating anything else? There is only one way: Allow for the possibility and imagine—or visualize—it happening. Around that basic statement can grow any number of techniques (see fallacy 94), but the techniques are simply methods to facilitate the process. They are not truths themselves. (I once read that it takes seventeen minutes of visualization to create a goal. Not sixteen or eighteen, but precisely seventeen. I often wonder if the author ever realized that the seventeen-minute "law" was her own belief, rather than a universal truth.)

Fallacy 85: Talking to myself is an innocent pastime.

EW THOUGHT . . . Here's some very interesting news that suggests there is nothing innocent or neutral about self-talk. Thoughts and the intent behind them produce an inner sound that passes through the body. The body then reacts to the intent wrapped into that inner sound. If we're feeling content with ourself, in love with life, then the inner sound kisses our cells with its clarity. And if we've been grousing all day about the god-awful job the plumber did in the downstairs bathroom, our anger or criticism becomes a flow of negativity throughout the body—and the body will react. A headache, perhaps? A pain in the neck? A knot in the stomach? Then add to our complaints anxiety about a burned rump roast, a late husband, a two-pound weight gain that morning, or simply a generalized fear, and we're well on our way to something more debilitating than a mere headache. Now extrapolate those kinds of thoughts and emotions over a week's time, or a month's, or a year's—or a lifetime's. Is it any wonder we knock ourselves out with the flu, create lumps where they shouldn't be, have "sudden" heart attacks?

Since thoughts and intent produce an inner sound that strongly affects our body, it's prudent to try to closely watch the flow of our thinking, and change our attitude, if called for. Of course, if we're on a jolly roll, and all's right in our world, our thoughts will automatically sustain us in good health. So learn to use positive verbal and mental suggestions to counter any negativity you may be feeling, and let the natural inner sound of your intent work for you, instead of against you.

Fallacy 86: Emotions should run their course.

EW THOUGHT . . . Emotions are extremely potent in the creative process. Often our expectations—that last rung on the creation ladder—spring from the emotions generated by our beliefs. Which means our emotions are key to forming our life's events. So, it would follow that it's extremely important for us to become aware of our emotions— both "negative" and "positive"—and rather than let them control us, learn to manage them. Not by stuffing them, as in, say, pretending we're happy when we're sad, but by redirecting our minds to more beneficial thoughts and beliefs . . . which will automatically initiate the emotions attached to them.

When Stan died, although I maintained a reasonable exterior, I was lost in an inner sea of grief. It's an awful place to be, and I knew within days that I had to either work with my emotions or reach depths of blackness no one should have to face. So, the first thing I did was refuse to use the word grief. "Deep sadness" replaced it in my vocabulary, because deep sadness had no personal or cultural beliefs attached to it, beliefs that reinforced what seemed a permanent loss, and beliefs that validated my right, if you will, to succumb to uncontrollable emotion.

The next thing I did was use some of the tools Stan had taught me for the year prior to his passing. He'd learned to change his emotions at will, transforming them from uneasy ones that would keep him down, to ones that would break the cycle. Simple tools, really. One thing I did was tell myself before sleep that tomorrow would be a happy day. Upon waking, I reminded myself of the same thought. While my days were far from happy for a while, that suggestion alone started me looking for the bright moment, the moment of clarity, the moment of peace, that perhaps I would have overlooked otherwise. And then at bedtime I built on my collected moments, recounting them in my mind, and trying to hold one to the point of sleep, hopefully taking it with me into the dream state where perhaps I could develop it further.

I also simply refused to allow certain emotions their due. While I didn't bully them out of my mind and body, I did move my thoughts from them. For instance, instead of wallowing in sweet memories that brought pain, I shifted to thoughts of a bright future, where no pain resided. And my emotions shifted accordingly.

Over the months, I experimented with my emotions and thoughts. And I am absolutely convinced my efforts paid off, in that I experienced a much shorter span of deep sadness than do most people who have lost a dearly beloved. One thought I held high throughout, that perhaps had the most significant impact on my emotions: Stan lives today as surely as he lived yesterday. He continues, because he is eternal consciousness. He explores, he experiences, he loves me from his broader perspective. And when I transition into consciousness without physical form, we will experience each other in ways only guessed at today.

Fallacy 87: Worry is a part of life.

EW THOUGHT . . . Worry is counterproductive. It assumes something is about to go wrong, so it usually does. Why? Because we've placed strong faith in that given outcome. Why focus on those types of probabilities? Why not set worry aside, tell yourself all will work out for everyone concerned, and go about your business? Allow new probabilities to develop that will offset the event you fear. Tell yourself that you'll not worry about the problem for the next day or week or month, that you'll keep an open mind to other solutions, and, most importantly, that you'll talk to your inner self about the situation and ask for guidance.

And don't forget to follow that guidance when it shows up!

By breaking the cycle of worry, I've seen computer problems suddenly solved without effort, divorces go smoothly, money arrive in time, illness curtailed. I've seen vacations from hell straighten out, gardens grow with fewer weeds, house construction flow easily, crucial meetings start on time. It's all about conscious choices, and the significance we place on those choices.

Fallacy 88: *If I follow my impulses, they lead me astray.*

 EW THOUGHT . . . True impulses don't lead to the spontaneous, irrational acts of, say, striking a blow to our neighbor or ramming the slow car ahead of us. In fact, explosive, aggressive, or hurtful acts are the result of impulses ignored. When we don't follow impulses spontaneously as we receive them, impulses that would help us dissipate our fear and anger as it arises, emotions build to the exploding point. Unfortunately, once we're burned by acts that seemed impulsive, we tend to assume that all impulses will lead to trouble—and further ignore them, only adding to the problem.

The solution: Take it nice and easy with impulses for a while. Acknowledge them, follow them with your thoughts, try to sense your inner feelings about them. Then, on a case by case basis, decide whether or not to follow individual impulses, and watch where the action, or non-action, leads you. We've all heard stories about the results of following an impulse, from finding a new love to mending fences within the family. And we've all heard tales of the rocky road walked after not following them, too. The bottom line is, when acted upon spontaneously, with trust, impulses will ultimately lead us to value fulfillment.

Fallacy 89: If I create my reality, then I create you.

EW THOUGHT . . . The physical representation of you in my space continuum is composed of my energy and brought into existence by my inner self. But, the essence and pattern of you is yours alone. I only "borrow" it from nonphysical reality, or the spacious present, where it resides. We are all nonphysical beings first and foremost, even if we don't remember the fact in the awake state, and no one can alter us substantially. But what each of us can do is choose which probable person we'll interact with by selecting them through our intent.

Life is a cooperative venture of massive proportions. When we need interaction with a consciousness for a specific reason, some consciousness will show up on our doorstep to fill the role—as the paper boy, for example, if we've signed up for the *Times*. If we see him physically, we've literally created him in our space continuum. If we don't, we've only created the paper, which we'll find lying on the doorstep when we open the door. In his own space continuum, the paper boy will have created our home, delivered our paper to our very physical doorstep, and moved on to the next event, without seeing, or creating, us.

There is no interaction with others that is not drawn into our life because of our thoughts, attitudes, emotions, focus, and intent. It matters not whether the event takes place on the job, at the grocery store, or in the privacy of our bedroom, the people simply would not be involved in our life unless we asked them to participate, and they agreed. The message, then, is very clear: If we're unhappy with the behavior of someone in our reality, it's up to us to change something in our own mind so the exterior interaction will change. That's not to say all will be love and light between us, but it is to say a resolution will be worked out that will be to the greater good of all involved.

Take a slothful employee, for example. True, we brought her into our reality for private reasons—perhaps we wish to hone our management skills, or maybe part of our life's purpose is to learn to control our emotions and keep a clear head. But it is also true we don't necessarily need to work with her on her slothfulness. By changing our attitude toward her, perhaps we'll draw in a probable employee who realizes her job is on the line, so she cleans up her act. Or, we might draw in a probable employee who we end up firing, because it's the only resolution that seems indicated. Either way, we'll solve our dilemma. And if we handle it properly, it will be to everyone's greater good, even if that greater good isn't readily apparent.

So, how do we work such magic? We start by understanding that the other person is consciousness playing a role for us.

Then, we cut them some slack because of it. We go into an altered state and ask to meet with that consciousness and work things out. We see ourselves smiling at each other, both of us knowing quite well that our little physical drama is just an act we're involved in for each other's sake. We agree we'll end the play soon, and we'll trust our inner selves to help put the probabilities in place that will make it happen. Then, in physical reality, we'll make our decisions and choices, keeping in mind what occurred in our altered state. And though we may end up firing the person, we'll treat them with integrity and simple regard throughout the process. In our mind, we'll wish them the best out of life.

When communications are psychically open between people, a more constructive energy is available—not simply psychologically speaking, but more importantly, metaphysically speaking. There is literally a different composition of characteristics to an energy that is in rapport with another, versus one that is not. We can use that energy to our great advantage in all sorts of situations—if, that is, we understand the nature of reality.

Fallacy 90: Since I create my own reality, I get whatever I ask for.

 EW THOUGHT . . . Let's clarify who "I" refers to in both parts of the statement, "Since I create my own reality, I get whatever I ask for." The I in "Since I create my own reality" refers to the whole consciousness—the inner and outer "I." This "I" works as a unit to bring about the most fulfilling life possible for the outer self. The I in "I get whatever I ask for," on the other hand, refers solely to the outer self.

Not surprisingly, there are times when what the outer self wants is in direct conflict with what the inner self sees as the best move for the outer self. In that case, the inner self will try, in numerous ways, to talk the outer self out of its position. It will send suggestions for new directions to try, or other paths to take, possibly even showing the outer self, through the example of another person or an outside event, just what the end result might be unless a different road is chosen. The outer self might experience this input as indecision, or anxiety, or even physical discomfort. Something just won't feel right, or secure, to the outer self.

Two things can happen at this point. The inner self might step in and simply end the situation, taking away the possibility completely. Or, if the outer self plunges ahead, insisting through focus and intent, and despite obvious warnings, to pursue the goal, the inner self might throw up its hands and back off. Anybody care to guess what might happen to the outer self once its forced goal is reached? Anybody been in that position? Anybody want to do it again?

The solution is rather apparent. If we're at all uncomfortable with a goal or choice we're about to make, we need to first look at our beliefs around the subject. If they feel fine, as if there is no obvious reason we'd meet conflict over our choice, beliefs probably aren't the cause of our uneasiness. We might then approach the situation internally during an altered state and ask our inner self for clear guidance. We must keep in mind that our inner self has the bigger picture at its command, and if our goal doesn't come about this time, in spite of solid beliefs, there must be an overriding reason. As time progresses, watch for that reason. Watch for the event that will tell us why our inner self didn't think we should move in that direction after all.

And lest you're wondering about the depth of support offered by an inner self, there are times when our inner self will simply throw us a bonus, just because. Something wonderful will happen that seems to come from nowhere, and in spite of our beliefs. That's our inner self's way of making physical reality more fun and inspiring, and of showing us there's an alternate side to our normal beliefs that we may want to explore, so that fun and inspiration come more often into our life.

Fallacy 91: Another person can control my energy.

 EW THOUGHT . . . In a reality where one must be invited to participate in another's space continuum (as discussed in fallacy 89) it should be clear that no person can control our energy. Of course, for those who believe that others can control their energy, the idea holds great sway, and its validity is proven over and over to them.

If you hold such a belief and wish not to, try this. In an altered state, imagine the person who you fear is using energy to control you. Imagine them disappearing. Then, imagine them reappearing in your reality, but see your own personal energy fill in their pattern. And make sure you realize you're doing it in your own space continuum, your safe haven. Then, have the person give you the evil eye and thrust energy your way. Laugh at them, because the only energy they can force on you is your own! Now have them disappear once more, and consciously decide never to believe again that they can hurt you. And they can't.

Fallacy 92: Energy cannot be multiplied.

EW THOUGHT . . . There is a phenomenon that occurs when groups meet with a certain intent—a group energy develops that becomes more than its individual parts. It's not technically that the energy multiplies, but that the intent each participant holds magnifies the power of the energy present.

So, what can a group do with such power? Win a lottery. Form a company. Start a war. March for gay rights. Organize a family reunion. We use group energy all the time to create large, mass events. Our future mission, if we choose to accept it, then, is to learn to consciously harness the power within such energy to create a better world.

Fallacy 93: Ouija boards are of the dark side.

EW THOUGHT . . . By now you know there is no such thing as a dark side—unless you believe in it. So-called occult tools such as Ouija boards, then, are as neutral as the material from which they're manufactured. Like anything else, they'll become whatever we wish them to be, seeing that we're the gods that imbue them with meaning.

So, we can choose to believe they can be a great conduit between our outer self and inner self.

Actually, for ten years Stan and I talked, via the Ouija board, to what we called the "Committee"—the Committee being, so they said, a meshing of our inner selves. As I discuss in detail in *Ten Thousand Whispers,* the Ouija board is a quick, easy, pleasant, humorous, satisfying, insightful, helpful, creative way to meet your inner self face to face, or word to word. Simply start by finding a friend as curious as yourself, put your fingers on the plastic pointer, ask your question, keep an open mind—and use some discrimination with what you receive. If Santa Claus appears in spiritual robes, you might want to ask your inner self why it's playing that particular role. Be playful. Remember, the board will provide "light" if you believe it will. Or it will provide "darkness" if you believe it will.

Fallacy 94: Dreams are so spontaneous they can't be directed.

EW THOUGHT . . . Dreams are spontaneous, but they can be directed, to a degree. Certainly lucid dreaming proves so, as do conscious out-of-bodies from the dream state. Another way to direct a dream involves a prior request of your inner self. Ask your inner self for a dream relating to a specific topic. Do you want to experience the most vivid dream of your life? Then ask for it. Do you need serious help in solving a problem? Go ahead, request it. Do you wish to meet your future mate in the dream state? Give it a try. The dream state is a fertile ground supplied by your inner self for your conscious use. So go and do, and have fun with it.

Fallacy 95: I'm only playing mind games when I try to consciously create a goal.

EW THOUGHT . . . If we say cynically or in disbelief that we're only "playing mind games" when we try to create a goal, it suggests that we don't yet understand the power of the mind and the nature of reality. But there is an exciting world of truth to the notion that we're playing mind games. Cathleen and I saved this fallacy as the last one of the book, because it allows us to wrap up with a very potent conscious creation technique. Yes, it's true. We're simply playing mind games to create a goal. How else does one create a goal in this psychological medium called physical reality but by the use of the multidimensional mind?

To briefly reiterate the basics of creation, because we'll be using them in this technique: Thoughts and emotions are what eventually lead to the creation of events and material objects. Desire, which is focused emotion behind a thought, helps considerably. But nothing happens without some level of expectation backing the desire. Desire on its own isn't enough. Expectation or assumption that the event can and will occur is mandatory, as is the ability to sense or imagine it.

Okay, that's the formula for basic creation in the physical realm. But what we're attempting is *conscious* creation, and that takes another ingredient—trust. It's not as if conscious creation is an accepted mode of operation in today's world, with a zillion people hawking its virtues. That means we're pioneering the concept every time we give it a go—and that necessitates finding enough trust within ourselves to proceed, whether anybody else on the planet believes in it or not. Trust or faith also suggests to us that the very fabric of the universe supports our efforts, including our inner self, because that *is* the nature of reality.

Cathleen and I found that one of the most difficult issues with conscious creation is holding our goal in our mind's eye with enough clarity to allow it to develop in the field of probabilities. So, over time we devised a simple technique that combines thought, emotion, desire, intent, focus, imagination, expectancy, and trust, all in one sweet package, a package that can be easily and instantly established in our mind, when wanted or needed. Here it is, for you to use as you wish.

In your mind, to the left, create a waist-high solid wall that runs straight ahead for as far as you can see. On this wall are the words, "Nothing else is an option." To the right, create an identical wall. The words on this wall are, "Don't equivocate." Between the two walls create a wide road constructed of your compressed energy turned to light. This road you will call your Highway of Certainty.

That's the basic structure. You'll be using it for a myriad of circumstances, so practice creating it quickly—it's not meant to be a deep-trance technique, per se. Learn to throw it out there while you're driving to work, or while listening to music, or before sleep, or in an altered state of consciousness.

Now, let's say your goal is to create a new job. See yourself standing on your Highway of Certainty between your parallel walls. Say, "I have a new job." Then, look at the writing on the left wall, "Nothing else is an option," and close your mind down to any thought or feeling that suggests otherwise. Then, look to your right, at the words, "Don't equivocate," and close your mind down to any waffling you might be inclined toward. Feel your feet standing on your own energy, and know with trust that the outcome is yours to create, and that you've done just that. Now, add emotion to your picture by seeing fireworks above, in celebration of your new position, and feel great happiness. Or, see your wife running toward you on the Highway of Certainty, shouting, "Honey, they've called with a job offer!" and whoop and holler right along with her.

Do this little exercise often, especially when you feel your-self wavering for whatever reason. Then, as your creation builds energy in the field of probabilities, things will start happening in your daily world. Take action when an impulse arises or a stray thought enters your mind that suggests a certain direction be explored. Do the usual, too, such as sending out resumes. And, most importantly, make decisions as though the final goal is on the horizon and part of your given future.

What you're doing is creating the event in your mind so concretely that your inner self knows you'll accept no other op-tion, and that you're not equivocating on your desire. Then it's up to your inner self to take over and make the final scenario happen. Trust that it will. In fact, trust that your inner self will add its own energy to your desire, magnifying its strength in the field of probabilities far beyond what you could do alone, be-cause that's the nature of the inner self.

Trust also that you can heal your body with this tech-nique. The body is an ongoing event, so the same guidelines of conscious creation apply. And please don't take another person's word, medical expert or no, as the final say in defining the condition of your body. It's your body, not theirs. It's your inner self, not theirs. It's you who'll work to correct the problem.

Trust, trust, trust.

Solving the Problem With a Hissy Fit

The painters and other craftspeople had been around for weeks, bringing a controlled chaos to our home-under-renovation. That they were constantly underfoot didn't start getting on my nerves until late one afternoon near the end of the job. My attention was split in a dozen directions that day, and I wasn't in the mood for it. Just about the time I realized the painters were applying the wrong color to the hallway, the lights in the living room started intermittently blinking off and on. In between grabbing curious cats out of the way of paint cans and arguing my point with the painters, the thought crossed my mind that I'd have to get an electrician in to fix the old wiring in the living room the next morning, as it was too late to call them now.

That's when the lights really took off, blinking with a constant staccato that suggested a serious problem. I'd had it. I was alone in the living room, so

> I allowed myself some serious temper. "Damn it, stop that!" I hissed to the universe. Curiously, the lights blinked once or twice more, then stopped for the evening. They started again in the morning, but by then the electrician was on his way.

In Summary

The universe leans in our direction. No matter what the exterior world screams at us during trying events, the universe does indeed lean in our direction. The discrepancy between this truth and what we experience is caused by lack of knowledge about the nature of reality. When we realize how and why creation happens, it all starts to make sense—and we can ignore that most of the world still believes Darwin and Freud, because we know differently. And we're secure enough with our knowledge to apply it to our life, and monitor the results.

Since our reality is literally constructed anew with each moment that passes, it gives us the opportunity to play with supposedly immutable laws and alter their effects. From changing weather patterns to re-materializing lost jewelry, we're learning just how flexible this reality and its laws really are. And that flexibility includes the malleability of time. We now know, because all time is truly simultaneous, that we can play in the spacious present and redesign some of the events from our official past. We also know that we can go into the future and meet a future self. Or, if we prefer, that we can step beyond this lifetime into our past existences, learning about our self from a greater perspective.

Life is a web of ongoing significances which we translate into physicality from the vast field of probabilities. That's where patterns for all potential idea constructions reside, and once we turn our attention in a pattern's direction, it becomes probable that the pattern will enter our life. It's all a matter of focus, and what we give significance to via our thoughts, attitudes, and beliefs. Worry, for instance, is counterproductive, because it assumes a significance that, by nature, starts to build exactly that which we're worried about. And since our thoughts and intents produce an inner sound that passes through the body and affects it either negatively or positively, we may want to get worry and other negativity under control.

When we create a mental image in our mind, it's composed of invisible light, sound, and electromagnetic properties, just as is the pattern for a physical object. That means that the mental image is incipient matter and so will attempt to reproduce itself in physical reality. Which is why visualization is such a great tool for conscious creation, and why there is a definite connection between images and materialization.

Beliefs are nothing more than unquestioned assumptions. However, they form the framework around which our life is woven. It's virtually impossible to make obvious, sustained change to our life without altering our beliefs. It's not that beliefs are particularly difficult to change; it's that they're difficult to see at times because of their stature as "fact" in our mind. Usually they go unchallenged, accepted as truths. So altering a belief requires removing the significance we've assigned to it. We can do this in different ways, perhaps by using visualization to replace one belief with another, or simply by consciously rejecting a belief and insisting it's no longer an option in our life. No matter the technique we use to change beliefs, the bottom line is that over time we're removing or softening the significance we've assigned to the belief.

Behind every emotion is a belief. Emotions are extremely potent in the creative process because of the power inherent in them. They thrust beliefs forward into our life, usually with great impact. When we redirect our emotions, the beliefs that generated them tend to loosen, and even change. So, while it's not healthy to "stuff" emotions, it's very smart to deal with them up front, see them as the reflections of our beliefs, and move on.

While it's true that the physical representation of a person in our space continuum is composed of our energy and brought into existence by our inner self, the essence and pattern of that person is theirs alone. We only "borrow" it from nonphysical reality, or the spacious present, where it resides. However, being that it's our reality, we can choose the probable version of the person and insert that choice into our life. Better said, we can select how we want to live our life, what emotions we wish to hold, the clarity of mind we want to enjoy. That mindset will, in turn, draw certain people to us that will allow our life to reflect those thoughts and attitudes. So the lesson is that if we don't like our interaction with another person, we should strive to change our own mind about the situation, and that, in turn, will bring about a solution that is for the greater good of all concerned. In actuality it will draw in another probable version of the person, and that new version will be there as a part of the resolution.

While the phrase "I create my own reality" is true, it does not mean that the outer self, or ego, gets whatever it asks for. There are times when what the ego wants is in direct conflict with what the inner self sees as the most beneficial move for the ego. In that case, the inner self will either try to talk the ego out of the choice it's made, or it will close down the choice as an option. If the ego chooses to pursue its choice in spite of psychic or physical uneasiness, it pays the price and hopefully learns from the experience. However, there are times, too, when our inner self will send us a bonus event, one that bypasses our limiting beliefs and brings a touch of happiness with it. And when our desires need shoring up, our inner self will add its incredible energy to ours, magnifying our desires in the field of probabilities.

In a framework where one must be invited to participate in another's space continuum, it's not true that anyone can control our energy through psychic means. Unless we allow it, that is, because of our belief in their ability to do so. And on the subject of energy, it's very true that when a group of people focuses on a specific intent, the psychic force of the group magnifies into something greater than its parts. Some day we will understand far more about individual and group energy, and put each to sustained, conscious use.

There are many means by which to interact with our inner self—including following the impulses, intuition, and insights sent our way by a helpful inner self every day of our life. And we can use an altered state to access the deeper regions of our multidimensional consciousness and the action that takes place outside of time and space. But we can also connect with our inner self on a Ouija board, through automatic writing, by channeling, through a Tarot deck, et cetera, et cetera. And, of course we can use the dream state to receive guidance and direction.

When we choose to try conscious creation, we must keep several factors in mind. First, thoughts and emotions are what eventually lead to the manifestation of an event or material object. Desire helps, too. But nothing happens without some level of expectation stirred into the pot. Expectation or assumption is mandatory, along with a good, healthy dollop of trust—in ourself, and in our inner self. Then we can create techniques, such as the one described in fallacy 95, that can assist us in the conscious creative process, helping us bring the good things of life to our psychic doorstep.

All in all, we live in one fine reality. It's a place that supports our desires, helps us to learn to manipulate energy, and leads us to value fulfillment. And it's our job to understand its nature so that we can stop haphazardly creating events and learn, instead, to finesse our creations into ones worthy of lower-case gods in a physical environment.

Moving On . . . And Bringing It Home

There is no magic wand available to us, from our inner self or otherwise, that allows us to create the kind of life we wish to experience. There are, however, magical thoughts, attitudes, and beliefs that allow us to do so. So as we reach the end of *Fallacies*, Cathleen and I would like to leave you with a few key points that we think will help you hold the mindset crucial to consciously creating your experiences. We thank you for joining us on this journey and wish you all the best in your quest to consciously create a more fulfilling, magical life.

> ✦ Faith is an active ingredient. Once you cultivate some faith in yourself and your ability to consciously interact with the universe, you yield far more than you sow.

➔ It's important to realize your desire is being developed in the field of probabilities, whether or not you see immediate results. This is where faith comes in.

➔ Energy is not neutral. It's a positive force, ever inclined toward creativity and fulfillment. So, in the field of probabilities there are no impediments to those desires that would naturally lead to a fulfilling life.

➔ Since those desires that lead to fulfillment are more in keeping with the natural leanings of the field of probabilities, they grab hold more quickly.

➔ Your inner self automatically adds its own magnification to your desires. So, once you get rolling, the acceleration can be astounding.

➔ Besides stating your clear intent, having faith in the process, leaving the means and details to your inner self, you have simply to relax and refrain from worrying as much as possible.

➔ As you continue your efforts to fulfill your desires, you attract from the field of probabilities everything you need to flesh out those desires.

➔ Allow for no options to your desires, and don't equivocate on the outcome.

➔ To improve the timing around your desire, TRUST.

➔ The energy used to create your desire will spill over into other areas of your life, and beneficial results will surface there, also.

➔ The more you enjoy life and your daily moments, the less difficulty you will have in any area. So, make one of your primary goals to appreciate life to its fullest.

➔ There is a strong desire by your inner self to help you be happy. Know you have a very influential support team behind you.

➔ Think, trust, expect, receive. There is no more practical or magical process in the universe. Make good use of it!

LOOK FOR THESE BOOKS
PUBLISHED BY THE WOODBRIDGE GROUP
NOW AVAILABLE THROUGH
MOMENT POINT PRESS

BY LYNDA DAHL

Beyond the Winning Streak
Using Conscious Creation to
Consistently Win at Life
(book and audio versions)

Ten Thousand Whispers
A Guide to Conscious Creation
(book and audio versions)

The Wizards of Consciousness
Making the Imponderable Practical

BY NORMAN FRIEDMAN

Bridging Science and Spirit
Common Elements in David Bohm's
Physics, the Perennial Philosophy, and Seth
(book and audio versions)

The Hidden Domain
Home of the Quantum Wave
Function, Nature's Creative Source

About the Authors

After working for companies such as Apple Computer, Lynda Dahl ended her corporate career as a vice president in the computer industry. She is listed in the *Who's Who Registry of Global Business Leaders*. She now writes and lectures extensively on consciousness and has appeared on countless radio and television programs. She is also the president and co-founder of Seth Network International. She lives in Eugene, Oregon.

Cathleen Kaelyn, Lynda Dahl's daughter, is an audiotape voice talent and stage and screen actor. She has been nominated three times for the prestigious Irene Ryan Acting Award. She lives in Sherman Oaks, California, with her husband, actor Scott Rinker.

For information regarding speaking engagements
and to contact the authors, please
write, phone, or email
Moment Point Press
PO Box 4549
Portsmouth, NH 03802
Phone: (207) 438-9101
Toll Free: (800) 556-1828
info@momentpoint.com

www.momentpoint.com